I
MUST WIN THIS
BATTLE

(MORE THAN 2000 LIFE CHANGING PRAYER POINTS)

TIMOTHY ATUNNISE

TSA SOLUTION PUBLISHING
ATLANTA, GEORGIA

I MUST WIN THIS BATTLE

Copyright © 2011 by Timothy Atunnise

Unless otherwise specified, all Scripture quotations in this book are from The Holy Bible, King James Version. KJV is Public domain in the United States printed in 1987.

Timothy Atunnise
GLOVIM PUBLICATIONS
Global Vision Ministries Inc.
1096 Bethsaida Road
Riverdale, GA 30296 USA.
info@glovimonline.org
www.glovimonline.org

TSA Solution Publishing
A division of Timat Store, LLC.
Atlanta, GA 30294
timatstore@yahoo.com

Cover Design: Tim Atunnise

ISBN 978-1-4611-5783-0

Printed in the United States of America

DEDICATION

This book is dedicated to my boys, Timothy and Joseph, who spent all their Spring break that is designed for them to rest and play to type the manuscript of this book and make the availability possible at the time promised.
You are precious! May the Lord continue to increase you in wisdom, and in every knowledge in the name of Jesus Christ.

To my Lord Jesus Christ:
Thank you for the mercy and grace you extend to someone like me.

IMPORTANT NOTICE

Deliverance is a benefit of the Kingdom, only for the children of God. If you have not accepted Jesus Christ as your personal Lord and Savior, this is the best time to do so.

Before you continue, you need to be sure you are in the right standing with God if you want to exercise authority and power in the name of Jesus Christ. The Bible says,

"Then he called his twelve disciples together, and gave them power and authority over all devils, and to cure diseases." - Luke 9:1

"And these signs shall follow them that believe; in my name shall they cast out devils; they shall speak with new tongues; they shall take up serpents; and if they drink any deadly thing, it shall not hurt them; they shall lay hands on the sick, and they shall recover." – Mark 16:17-18.

These are promises for the Children of God, not just for everyone. Why don't you give your life to Christ today and you will have access to the same promises. Food that is meant for the children will not be given to the dogs.

"But he answered and said, it is not meet to take the children's bread, and cast it to dogs" – Matthew 15:26.

If you really want to be delivered from any bondage of the wicked and be set free from any form of captivity, I ask you today to give your life to Christ. If you are ready, say this prayer with all your heart:

"Dear Heavenly Father, You have called me to Yourself in the name of Your dear Son Jesus Christ. I realize that Jesus Christ is

the only Way, the Truth, and the Life.
I acknowledge to You that I am a sinner. I believe that Your only begotten Son Jesus Christ shed His precious blood on the cross, died for my sins, and rose again on the third day. I am truly sorry for the deeds which I have committed against You, and therefore, I am willing to repent (turn away from my sins). Have mercy on me, a sinner. Cleanse me, and forgive me of my sins.

I truly desire to serve You, Lord Jesus. Starting from now, I pray that You would help me to hear Your still small voice. Lord, I desire to be led by Your Holy Spirit so I can faithfully follow You and obey all of Your commandments. I ask You for the strength to love You more than anything else so I won't fall back into my old ways. I also ask You to bring genuine believers into my life who will encourage me to live for You and help me stay accountable.

Jesus, I am truly grateful for Your grace which has led me to repentance and has saved me from my sins. By the indwelling of Your Holy Spirit, I now have the power to overcome all sin which before so easily entangled me. Lord Jesus, please transform my life so that I may bring glory and honor to You alone and not to myself.

Right now I confess Jesus Christ as the Lord of my life. With my heart, I believe that God the Father raised His Son Jesus Christ from the dead. This very moment I acknowledge that Jesus Christ is my Savior and according to His Word, right now I am born again. Thank You Jesus, for coming into my life and hearing my prayer. I ask all of this in the name of my Lord and Savior, Jesus Christ. Amen".

I hereby congratulate and welcome you into the Kingdom. You hereby have full access to the benefits, promises and blessings of the Kingdom.

This book is loaded with blessings, you will not be disappointed as you continue to enjoy the goodness of the Lord.

INSTRUCTIONS

If you are new to this method of prayer, please follow this instruction carefully:

Step 1:

Spend enough time in praising and worshiping God not just for what He is about to do or what He has done, but WHO HE IS.

Step 2:

Unforgiveness will surely hinder your prayer, take time to remember all those who have done you wrong, and forgive them from the bottom of your heart. THIS IS VERY IMPORTANT BECAUSE YOUR DELIVERANCE DEPENDS ON IT.

Step 3:

Believe in your heart that God will answer your prayer when you call upon Him, and do not doubt in your heart.

Step 4:

Pray in the name of Jesus Christ alone.

Step 5:

Repeat each prayer point 25 to 30 times or until you are convinced that you receive answer before you go to the next prayer point. **Example:** When you take prayer point number 1, you say this prayer over and over again, 25 – 30 times or until you are convinced that you have an answer before you go to prayer point number 2.

Step 6:

It will be more effective if you can fast along with your prayer. If you want total deliverance from your bondage, take 3 days of sacrifice in fasting as you say your prayer aggressively, asking your situation to receive permanent solution and YOUR DELIVERANCE WILL BE MADE PERFECT IN THE NAME OF JESUS CHRIST. AMEN!

Table of Contents

BEFORE YOU START YOUR DAY

Passages To Read Before You Pray:
Psalms 23, 91, Isaiah 60:1-22

PRAYER POINTS:

1. Father Lord, I thank you for this great privilege to see another brand new day.
2. I will not go out today with the burden of sins upon my life, Father Lord, forgive me and cleanse me in the blood of Jesus Christ.
3. I cover myself and my household in the blood of Jesus Christ.
4. As I am going out today and when I am coming back home, I cover my car in the blood of Jesus Christ.
5. For my sake, roads are blessed in the name of Jesus Christ.
6. O God my Father, grant me angelic escort wherever I go today.
7. Today I reject any form of accident in the name of Jesus Christ.
8. Today I reject bad news, I shall receive good news from every area in the name of Jesus Christ.
9. I command this day to cooperate with the plan of God for me in the name of Jesus Christ.
10. I command this day to bring me joy and great success in the name of Jesus Christ.
11. Every uncompleted project in my life shall be completed today in the name of Jesus Christ.
12. Every situation will favor me today in the name of Jesus Christ.
13. Every circumstance will favor me today in the name of Jesus Christ.

14. I command this day to provide solution to my situations in the name of Jesus Christ.
15. Today every man and woman will go out of their way to do me good in the name of Jesus Christ.
16. Today I shall operate under open heavens in the name of Jesus Christ.
17. All things shall work together for my good today in the name of Jesus Christ.
18. Today I will receive favor in the sight of those who will decide on my advancement in the name of Jesus Christ.
19. I receive immunity against failure, I cannot fail today because Jesus is my Lord.
20. I command this day to speak prosperity into my life in the name of Jesus Christ.
21. I command this day to speak abundance into every area of my life in the name of Jesus Christ.
22. I receive anointing for greatness today.
23. Today I will run and not be weary, walk and not faint, I will mount up with wings as eagles in the name of Jesus Christ.
24. Today I will excel in every area of my life in the name of Jesus Christ.
25. Whatever I do today shall prosper in the name of Jesus Christ.
26. Today I will not disappoint God.
27. Today I will not disappoint my family and friends.
28. Today I will not disappoint myself.
29. Today I receive anointing and the grace of God to achieve great things in the name of Jesus Christ.
30. Where everybody fails today, I will not fail in the name of Jesus Christ.
31. I command you this day, you will not work against me in the name of Jesus Christ.

32. Every plan of the enemy against me today, I render null and void in the name of Jesus Christ.
33. I cancel every satanic attack planned for me today in the name of Jesus Christ.
34. O God my Father, increase your grace upon my life today.
35. Today O Lord, give me every reason to rejoice and celebrate in the name of Jesus Christ.
36. People that you have prepared to help me, Father Lord, let them locate me today.
37. People that you have prepared to contribute to my success, Father Lord, let them locate me today.
38. Today I receive power to prosper in the name of Jesus Christ.
39. Today I speak restoration into every area of my life in the name of Jesus Christ.
40. I will come home today celebrating and testifying in the name of Jesus Christ.

BEFORE YOU GO TO BED

Passages To Read Before You Pray:
Psalms 23, 42, 59, 91, 125

PRAYER POINTS:

1. Father Lord, I thank you for what you have done for me today.
2. Father Lord, I thank you for always being there for me even when I do not know it.
3. On the basis of your mercy O Lord, forgive me of all my sins and wrong doings in the name of Jesus Christ.
4. I cover myself and my household in the blood of Jesus Christ.
5. I draw the bloodline to surround my family and my property in the name of Jesus Christ.
6. No evil shall come near my family in the name of Jesus Christ.
7. No danger shall come near my dwelling place in the name of Jesus Christ.
8. I am well covered and protected in the Lord and by the power of His might.
9. I reject every dream attack in the name of Jesus Christ.
10. I reject nightmares in the name of Jesus Christ.
11. You power of the night, I am not your candidate, I cast you away from me in the name of Jesus Christ.
12. Every satanic dream designed to destroy destiny, I am not your candidate, be destroyed by the fire of God.
13. Every satanic dream designed to steal blessings, I am not your candidate, be destroyed by the fire of God.
14. Every satanic dream designed to plant sickness, you have no authority over my life, be destroyed by the fire of God.

15. Every night caterer feeding people in the dream, I do not need your service, die by the fire of God.
16. Every satanic agent having sex with people in their dreams, you have no authority over my soul and body, die by the fire of God.
17. Evil animals manifesting in my dreams, I condemn you tonight, die by the fire of God.
18. O God my Father, fight for me tonight and give me victory in the name of Jesus Christ.
19. Every satanic dream designed to confuse me, you will not prosper, be destroyed by the fire of God.
20. Bless me in my sleep tonight O Lord, as you have promised in your Word.
21. In my sleep tonight O Lord, give me a new revelation of your greatness in the name of Jesus Christ.
22. In my sleep tonight O Lord, give me a new revelation of your glory.
23. In my sleep tonight O Lord, show me the next step to take in life so that I will not miss my way.
24. In my sleep tonight O Lord, perform surgical operation and remove anything that can cause sickness in my body.
25. In my sleep tonight O Lord, demonstrate your power and uproot any tree that you did not plant in my life.
26. In my sleep tonight O Lord, give me direction about what to do with my life and how to do it in the name of Jesus Christ.
27. In my sleep tonight O Lord, restore back to me every good thing that enemies have stolen away from me in the name of Jesus Christ.
28. Tonight I shall have a good sleep in the name of Jesus Christ.
29. Every power taking sleep away from me, loose your hold over my life in the name of Jesus Christ.
30. In my sleep tonight O Lord, reveal unto me the deepest secret of my enemies.

31. Bless me tonight O Lord with divine revelation.
32. Every power turning my sleep into a battle field, die by the fire of God.
33. Every power that erases my memory before I wake up, you no longer have power over me, loose your hold over my life now in the name of Jesus Christ.
34. Every power using other people's images to attack me in the dream, die by the fire of God.
35. Satanic snakes manifesting in my dreams, die by the fire of God.
36. Every power that puts evil marks on my body in the night, die by the fire of God.
37. Every power pressing me in my sleep, die by the fire of God.
38. I will wake up rejuvenated, ready to fulfill purpose in the name of Jesus Christ.
39. As I am going to bed, Father Lord, surround me with your angels in the name of Jesus Christ.
40. I will wake in the morning with joy in my heart, songs of praise in my mouth, and testimonies in my life in the name of Jesus Christ.

DELIVERANCE FROM EVIL COVENANTS

Passages To Read Before You Pray:
Psalms: 2, 18, 30, 55, 68, 69, 94

PRAYER POINTS:
1. Every evil covenant that I have ignorantly made, I hereby renounce you, be nullified now.
2. Every evil covenant that anyone has made on my behalf, I renounce you, be nullified by the blood of Jesus.
3. Evil covenant of untimely death upon my life, I renounce you, be nullified by the blood of Jesus.
4. Any covenant that I have made with the devil or any evil spirit, I renounce you today, be nullified by the blood of Jesus.
5. Every covenant that I have made with the spirit of failure, I renounce you, be nullified by the blood of Jesus.
6. Any covenant that I have made with the spirit husband/wife, I renounce you, be nullified by the blood of Jesus.
7. Every covenant that I have ignorantly made by consulting psychic or any medium, be nullified by the blood of Jesus.
8. Every covenant that I have ignorantly made through sex outside marriage, be nullified by the blood of Jesus.
9. Every covenant that I have made through satanic initiation, be nullified by the blood of Jesus.
10. Every covenant that I have ignorantly made by wearing another person's outfit, be nullified by the blood of Jesus.
11. Every covenant that I have made through vain promises, be nullified by the blood of Jesus.
12. Every evil covenant made in my dreams, be nullified by the blood of Jesus.

13. Every covenant that I have ignorantly made with poverty, be nullified by the blood of Jesus.
14. Every covenant that I have made with sickness, be nullified by the blood of Jesus.
15. Every covenant that I have ignorantly made through worldly songs, I renounce you, be nullified by the blood of Jesus.

BATTLE OF THE MIND

Passages To Read Before You Pray:
Proverbs 23:7; 24:9; 15:26, Psalms 94:11; 64:6, Matthew 9:4; 15:19

PRAYER POINTS

1. Father Lord, I thank you for your faithfulness and kindness that you show me every day.
2. O God my Father, forgive me of all my sins and cleanse me of all unrighteousness according to your Word in the name of Jesus Christ.
3. O God my Father, purify my heart and give me grace to renew my mind daily in the name of Jesus Christ.
4. I cover my mind in the precious blood of Jesus Christ.
5. Any problem that I created in my mind that is now manifesting in the physical, Father Lord, deliver me and set me free in the name of Jesus Christ.
6. Every self-inflicted failure upon my life, I command you to end right now in the name of Jesus Christ.
7. Any area that I have put my life on hold through the thought of my mind, Father Lord, let there be divine intervention and let my life move forward in the name of Jesus Christ.
8. O God my Father, replace my unbelief with unshakable faith in the name of Jesus Christ.
9. O God my Father, by the authority given me in the name of Jesus Christ, I cast down every stronghold built against me through the thoughts of my mind.
10. Every evil thought of my mind that brings more problems into my life, I command you to flee and let my mind be filled with testimonies and thanksgiving in the name of Jesus Christ.

11. My mind is not a junkyard, I reject every evil thought dumped in my mind in the name of Jesus Christ.
12. Anything that will make me sin against you, Father Lord, let it be completely erased from my memory in the name of Jesus Christ.
13. Anything in my mind that can lead me into captivity, Father Lord, let it be completely erased from my memory in the name of Jesus Christ.
14. Any spirit, power or personality that is using my mind as a gateway to control my life, I command you in the name of Jesus Christ, loose you hold over my life.

BREAKING THE YOKE OF DEBT

Passages To Read Before You Pray:
2 Kings 4:1-7, Deuteronomy 28:12

PRAYER POINTS

1. Father Lord, I thank you for the privilege to know you.
2. Father, forgive me of any sins that puts me in debt.
3. I cover myself, my household and my finances in the blood of Jesus.
4. O God my Father, deliver me by your power from bondage of debt that I put myself into.
5. O God my Father, deliver me by your power from bondage of debt originated from bad economy.
6. Every yoke of debt upon my life, you have no right to be there, break in Jesus name.
7. Every arrow of debt shot at me by the enemy, come out with all roots and go back to sender.
8. O God my Father, open unto me the flood gate of heaven, and pour down prosperity upon my life.
9. You spirit of debt, I reject you and cast you out of my life.
10. You spirit of debt, loose your hold over my life.
11. Every covenant of debt over my life, I terminate you now.
12. Release into my life O Lord, blessing that will put debt to shame.
13. O God my Father, let there be permanent separation between me and debt.
14. Lord, let there be a miracle that will eliminate all my debts.
15. You spirit of debt, I renounce you and I command you to leave and never come back.
16. Spirit of debt, you will have no control over my life.

17. I will be the lender and not the borrower.
18. Any situation in my life that will put me in debt receive solution now.
19. Any situation around me that will make me to borrow, receive solution now.
20. Open unto me O Lord, the good treasure of heaven.
21. O God my Father, bless the works of my hands in the name of Jesus Christ.

BREAKING UNGODLY SOUL-TIES

Passages To Read Before You Pray:
Psalms: 30, 55, 59

PRAYER POINTS

1. Father Lord, have mercy upon me today and forgive me of my sins that hold me captive.
2. I cover myself in the precious blood of Jesus.
3. I renounce every past and present ungodly relationship, and I invite Jesus into my life today.
4. By the power in the blood of Jesus, I break every ungodly soul ties in the name of Jesus.
5. Today I break every ungodly soul ties between me and any man or woman, living or dead in the name of Jesus Christ.
6. Let the blood of Jesus flush away every strange blood flowing in my body.
7. Let the blood of Jesus flush away every backwardness that enters my life through ungodly soul ties.
8. Let the blood of Jesus flush away every stagnation that enter into my life through ungodly soul ties.
9. Let the blood of Jesus flush away all sickness that enter into my life through ungodly soul ties
10. Let the blood of Jesus flush away all failure that enter into my life through ungodly soul ties
11. Let the blood of Jesus flush away lack and poverty that enter into my life through ungodly soul ties
12. Every problem that I have received through ungodly soul ties, I command you to be destroyed.
13. Any problems manifesting in my life as a result of ungodly soul ties I command you to be destroyed.

14. Any curse manifesting in my life as a result of ungodly soul ties, be nullified.
15. Any power that holds me captive because of ungodly soul ties, loose me and let me go.
16. Any agent of darkness that holds me captives because of ungodly soul ties, loose me and let me go.
17. My destiny that has been caged because of ungodly soul ties, I release you today.
18. My glory that has been covered because of ungodly soul ties be released today.
19. Power to succeed that has been taken away from me because of ungodly soul ties, I recover you today.
20. Power to prosper that is taken away from me because of ungodly soul ties, I recover you today.
21. Power to fulfill purpose, that is taken away from me because of ungodly soul ties, I recover you today.
22. Power to produce that is taken away from me because of ungodly soul ties, I recover you today.
23. Every demonic access into my life because of ungodly soul ties, I block it by the blood of Jesus Christ.
24. Every demonic access to my glory because of ungodly soul ties, I block it by the blood of Jesus.
25. Every satanic access to my marriage because of ungodly soul ties, I block it by the blood of Jesus.
26. Every demonic access to my finance because of ungodly soul ties, I block it by the blood of Jesus.
27. I break every evil covenant that I have made with anyone, living or dead.
28. I terminate every evil agreement that I have signed with anyone, living or dead.
29. Every ungodly union between me and anyone, in the past or in present, I annul it today.

30. Every past mistake that's still haunting me, loose me now and let me go.

DELIVERANCE FROM THE SCOURGE OF TONGUE

Passages To Read Before You Pray:
Proverbs 18:21; 13:3; 21:23, Matthew 12:36, 37; James 3:5,6

PRAYER POINTS

1. Father Lord, I thank you for being a good and wonderful Father.
2. Any problem in my life as a result of the words of my mouth, forgive me and deliver me in the name of Jesus Christ.
3. Any word that I have spoken in the past that enemies are now using against me, Father Lord, forgive me and nullify the effects in the name of Jesus Christ.
4. Any word that I have spoken in the past that is now haunting me, Father Lord, forgive me and set me free in the name of Jesus Christ.
5. Any area of life that I am creating more problems for myself through the words of my mouth, Father Lord, deliver me and help me to control my tongue in the name of Jesus Christ.
6. Any area that I have been fueling my problem through the words of my mouth, Father Lord, deliver me and help me to control my tongue in the name of Jesus Christ.
7. Any unjust word that I have spoken against the innocent, Father Lord, forgive me and deliver me in the name of Jesus Christ.
8. Father Lord, any word that I have spoken against you and your anointed, forgive me and deliver me in the name of Jesus Christ.
9. Any area that I am inviting enemies into my life by the words of my mouth, Father Lord, deliver me and help me to control my tongue in the name of Jesus Christ.

10. Any negative word that I have spoken against myself, that is now manifesting, Father Lord, forgive me and nullify the effects in the name of Jesus Christ.
11. Any negative word that I have spoken against anyone, that is now manifesting in my life, Father Lord, forgive me and nullify the effects in the name of Jesus Christ.

DIVINE OPPORTUNTY

Passages To Read Before You Pray:
1 Corinthians 16:9, Joel 2:25, Psalm 92

PRAYER POINTS

1. Father Lord , I thank you because your joy will always be my strength.
2. Anything that I have done, that will make me miss or lose my divine opportunity, forgive me O Lord.
3. Open unto me O Lord, a great door of opportunity that no one can shut.
4. Open unto me O Lord, an effective door of opportunity that cannot fail.
5. Any power fighting to rob me of my divine opportunity, I condemn you in the name of Jesus Christ.
6. Every lost opportunity, Father Lord, restore them back unto me.
7. Doors of opportunity that will lead me to greatness open them unto me O Lord.
8. Doors of opportunity to connect me with my divine helpers open them unto me O Lord.
9. Doors of opportunity that will change my life for good forever open them unto me O Lord.
10. Doors of opportunity that will lead to my breakthrough open them unto me O Lord.
11. Doors of opportunity that will lead me to an outstanding success open them unto me O Lord.
12. Doors of opportunity that will lead me to meeting people you have designed to contribute to my success open them unto me O Lord.

GATES OF HELL SHALL NOT PREVAIL AGAINST ME

Passages To Read Before You Pray:
Psalm 3; 24; 35; 69; 109, Luke 9:1, Revelation 12:11

PRAYER POINTS

1. Father Lord, I thank you for giving me victory over all powers of darkness.
2. Today O Lord, forgive me of all my sins and cleanse me in the blood of Jesus.
3. I cover myself and my household in the blood of Jesus.
4. O God my Father, expose and destroy every agent of darkness assigned against me, in the name of Jesus.
5. By the authority in the name of Jesus, I cancel every satanic assignment against my life and my household.
6. O God my Father, withdraw your grace that is covering agents of darkness assigned against my life, in Jesus' name.
7. Let the unquenchable fire of God be released upon agents of darkness working against me, in the name of Jesus.
8. Agents of darkness manifesting as angels of light in every area of my life, I release fire of destruction upon you, in the name of Jesus.
9. Any direct agent of hell working against me, I release fire of destruction upon you, in the name of Jesus.
10. Every indirect agent of hell (Contract agent) working against me, I release fire of destruction upon you, in the name of Jesus.
11. The gates of hell shall not prevail against me and my household, in the name of Jesus.

12. Any man or woman selling me and my household to any agent of darkness, I release fire of destruction upon you, in the name of Jesus.
13. Any plan of darkness to pollute my prayer altar, be terminated in the name of Jesus.
14. Any plan of darkness to contaminate my prayer altar, be terminated in the name of Jesus.
15. Every satanic virus working to cause damage in any area of my life, be destroyed by the fire of God.
16. Every satanic virus working to intercept what God is doing in my life, be destroyed by the fire of God in the name of Jesus.
17. Every satanic virus assigned to corrupt the anointing of God upon my life, be destroyed by the fire of God in the name of Jesus.
18. Every satanic virus sent to steal and to destroy me, receive destruction in the name of Jesus.
19. Any agent of hell working to create confusion in any area of my life, receive destruction in the name of Jesus.
20. Every satanic virus assigned to infect all the faithful around me, receive destruction in the name of Jesus.
21. Father Lord, let the fire of destruction locate and destroy every satanic virus assigned against me, in the name of Jesus.
22. Father Lord, let the fire of destruction locate and destroy every agent of hell working against my destiny in the name of Jesus.
23. Father Lord, let the fire of destruction locate and destroy every agent of confusion working against me, in the name of Jesus.
24. When enemies come like flood against me and my household, Lord, lift your standard for their destruction in the name of Jesus.
25. Jesus Christ, you are the Rock of Ages, crush every agent of darkness working against my peace in the name of Jesus.

26. Jesus Christ, you are the Rock of Ages, crush every power of darkness working against my progress in the name of Jesus.
27. Jesus Christ, you are the Rock of Ages, crush every gate of hell working to destroy your plan for me and my household in the name of Jesus.
28. Every spirit of deception around me, I bind you and cast you away from me in the name of Jesus.
29. Spirit of fake submission and fake humility among people around me, I bind you and cast you out in the name of Jesus.
30. Today O Lord, destroy every stronghold of the devil built against me in the name of Jesus.
31. Agents of destruction working against my home, Father Lord, expose them and destroy them in the name of Jesus.
32. No matter the activity of the enemy, my life shall move forward in the name of Jesus.
33. Every mouth speaking evil against me, you are condemned in the name of Jesus.
34. Every mouth spreading evil report about my life, you are condemned in the name of Jesus.
35. Every evil network working against me and my household, Father Lord, expose them and destroy them in the name of Jesus.
36. All agents of darkness manifesting as angels of light, Father Lord, expose them and destroy them in the name of Jesus.
37. All agents of stagnancy manifesting as angels of progress, Father Lord, expose them and destroy them in the name of Jesus.
38. All agents of trouble manifesting as angels of solution, Father Lord, expose them and destroy them in the name of Jesus.
39. O God my Father, release your fire into my life and my home and make me untouchable in the name of Jesus.
40. Lord Jesus, let the whole world know that you are my God in the name of Jesus.

GOD OF POSSIBILITY

Passages To Read Before You Pray:
Psalms: 18; 19; 30, Jeremiah 32:27, Luke 1:37

PRAYER POINTS

1. Father Lord, let your power deliver me from struggle of life.
2. In my life today O Lord, struggle is over.
3. O God my Father, soften my ground and let my land be fruitful.
4. Open my heaven today O Lord, and rain down your blessing upon m life.
5. Open my heaven today O Lord, and rain down abundance upon my life.
6. Open my heaven today O Lord, and release my breakthrough.
7. Open my heaven today O Lord, and confirm your Word in my life.
8. O God of possibility, demonstrate your power in my life.
9. O God of abundance, meet all my needs today.
10. O God my healer, heal my spirit, soul and body.
11. O God my Father, make me unstoppable no matter the efforts of my enemies.
12. O God Jehovah, make a way for me out of this wilderness of life.
13. O God my Father, let my joy and happiness be restored unto me.

THIS BATTLE

Passages To Read Before You Pray:
Exodus 14:14; 15:3; 23:27, 2 Chronicles 20:15-17, 32:8

PRAYER POINTS

1. Any sin in my life that can give my enemies legal ground in my life, forgive me and cleanse me.
2. I cover myself and my household in the blood of Jesus.
3. I equip myself with the whole armor of God.
4. I draw the bloodline around me and my household.
5. I claim back every legal ground that the enemy had claimed in my life in the name of Jesus Christ.
6. I render useless and ineffective, every strategy of the enemy using against me in the name of Jesus Christ
7. I render useless and ineffective, every weapon of the enemy fashioned against me in the name of Jesus Christ.
8. I render useless and ineffective, every weapon of the enemy fashioned against my destiny in the name of Jesus Christ.
9. I render useless and ineffective, every weapon of the enemy fashioned against my finances in the name of Jesus Christ.
10. I render useless and ineffective, every weapon of the enemy fashioned against my marriage in the name of Jesus Christ.
11. I render useless and ineffective, every weapon of the enemy fashioned against my health in the name of Jesus Christ.
12. I render useless and ineffective, every weapon of the enemy fashioned against my power to produce in the name of Jesus.
13. I render useless and ineffective, every weapon of the enemy fashioned against my children in the name of Jesus Christ.
14. Every battle rising against me from my father's house, O God Jehovah Nissi, fight and destroy them.

15. Every battle rising against me from my mother's house, O God Jehovah Nissi fight and destroy them.
16. Every battle rising against me from my in law's house, O God Jehovah Nissi fight and destroy them.
17. Every battle rising against me from unfriendly friends, O God Jehovah Nissi fight and destroy them.
18. Every battle rising against my children, O God Jehovah Nissi fight and destroy them.
19. Every battle rising against my progress, O God Jehovah Nissi fight and destroy them.
20. I claim victory over every battle of life in the name of Jesus.
21. Because Jesus is my commander –in-chief, I will not lose any battle.
22. Because Jesus is my commander-in-chief, I will win the battle over depression.
23. Because Jesus is my commander-in-chief, I will win the battle over poverty and lack.
24. Because Jesus is my commander-in-chief, I will win the battle over sickness and infirmity.
25. Because Jesus is my commander-in-chief, I will win the battle over barrenness and loneliness.
26. Because Jesus is my commander-in-chief, I will win the battle over every attack of the enemy.
27. Because Jesus is my commander-in-chief, I will win the battle over stagnation and backwardness.
28. Because Jesus is my commander-in-chief, I will win the battle attacking me in my mind.
29. Because Jesus is my commander-in-chief, I will win every battle attacking me to take my confidence.
30. Because Jesus is my commander-i- chief, I will win every battle attacking my spiritual life.
31. Because Jesus is my commander-in-chief, I will win every battle attacking my helpers.

32. I apply the blood of Jesus against every sickness in my body.
33. I apply the blood of Jesus against every devourer attacking my finances.
34. I apply the blood of Jesus to remove every shame and reproach.
35. I apply the blood of Jesus to erase every mark of the enemy upon my life.

I REFUSE TO CONTINUE LIKE THIS

Passages To Read Before You Pray:
1 Chronicles 4:9,10, Mark 5:25-34

PRAYER POINTS

1. Father Lord, I thank you for your grace and mercy.
2. Anything that I have done that gives enemy access to my life, forgive me today.
3. I neutralize the effect of food that I have eaten in the dream.
4. Every evil seed sown into my life through food in the dream, come out with all your poison in the name of Jesus Christ.
5. Every mouth broadcasting evil report about me, I silence you forever, and I condemn you in the name of Jesus Christ.
6. Every loop hole and crack in my wall, allowing the enemy to sneak into my life, I seal it up by the blood of Jesus.
7. Every contrary spirit and power that have sneaked into my life, Father Lord, destroy them by your fire.
8. Every serpentine spirit assigned against my life, Father Lord, destroy them by your fire.
9. Every serpentine spirit working to destroy the plan of God for me, be destroyed by the fire of God.
10. Every serpentine spirit planning to attack me, you cannot escape the judgment of God, be destroyed.
11. I get myself back on track from where my parents have put hold upon my life in the name of Jesus Christ.
12. You spirit of stagnancy, release me now, come out of my life with all your roots in the name of Jesus Christ.
13. You spirit of addiction, I cast you out of my life in the name of Jesus Christ.

14. Every spiritual bully, assigned against me to create fear and discouragement, Father Lord, destroy them.
15. You agent of darkness assigned against me, you will not escape the judgment of God.

I WILL GIVE BIRTH

Passages To Read Before You Pray:
Genesis 1:28, Exodus 23:26, Deuteronomy 7:14

PRAYER POINTS

1. Power to produce that enemy has taken away from me, I claim it back in the name of Jesus Christ.
2. As from this moment I will be productive, this is the Word of God concerning me.
3. Every dead organ in me, receive life now and produce in the name of Jesus Christ.
4. Every part of my body that has stop working, I command you get back to work.
5. I receive power to conceive and to deliver in the name of Jesus Christ.
6. I reject financial barrenness; I receive power to generate money in the name of Jesus Christ.
7. My business shall not be barren in the name of Jesus Christ.
8. My marriage shall not be barren in the name of Jesus Christ.
9. Anointing for multiplication, rest upon me now.
10. Anything that I have done in the past that hinder me from giving birth, forgive me Lord and nullify it.
11. Anything that enemy had done against me that hinder me from giving birth, forgive me Lord and nullify it.
12. Any covenant signed on my behalf that hinders me from giving birth, I nullify it in Jesus name.
13. Any covenant that I have ignorantly signed that hinder me from giving birth, be nullified in Jesus name.
14. Any mistake that I have made in the past that hinder me from giving birth, forgive me Lord and empower me to give birth.

15. Power to give birth that I have ignorantly traded away, Lord have mercy and redeem me.

LET THERE BE OPEN HEAVENS

Passages To Read Before You Pray:
Deuteronomy 28:12, Joel 2:22-24, Haggai 2:6-8

PRAYER POINTS

1. O God my Father, let there be open heavens over my life and my household.
2. O God my Father, let there be open heavens over my finances.
3. O God my Father, let there be open heavens over my business, ministry, and all sources of income.
4. O God my Father, let there be open heavens over this prayer meeting tonight.
5. O God my Father, let there be open heavens over my ministry
6. O God my father, open the flood gates of heaven and release the former and latter rain upon my life.
7. Father Lord, let every desert area of my life become fertile.
8. Father Lord, let every barren land in my life become fruitful.
9. Father Lord, let every curse upon my land be broken.
10. Father Lord, let every curse upon my life be broken.
11. Father Lord, let every evil expectation over my life be disappointed.
12. Let my harvest begin right now in the name of Jesus Christ.
13. I put an end to drought in my life today O God my Father.
14. Every seed of greatness deposited in me come alive in the name of Jesus Christ.
15. O God the consuming fire, let your fire destroy every evil agenda against my life.
16. O God the consuming fire, let your fire destroy every power closing my heavens.

17. I release the fire of God to destroy every power assigned to frustrate me.
18. I release the fire of God to destroy every power assigned to rob me of my blessing.
19. I release the fire of God to destroy every power assigned to hinder my miracles.
20. I release the fire of God to destroy every power assigned to delay my breakthrough.
21. Release your fire O Lord, and destroy my enemies round about.
22. Any power assigned to constantly increase my pain, O God my Father, destroy them by your fire.
23. Any powers assigned to constantly refuel my problem, O God my Father destroy them by your fire.
24. O God my Father, open the fire gates of Heaven and release my financial breakthrough.
25. Any power attacking my finances, O God my Father, release your fire and destroy them.
26. Every power and spirit of devourer against my finances, O God destroy them by your fire.
27. Open the heavens today O Lord, and let there be solution to every problem in my life.
28. Open the heavens O Lord, and let your favor overshadow every area of my life.
29. Open the Heavens O Lord, and let anointing of ease rest upon every area of my life.
30. Open the Heavens O Lord, and let every cloud of failure clear away.
31. Open the Heavens O Lord, and let every disappointment turn into blessings for me.
32. Open the Heavens O Lord, and let every shame in my life turn into manifestation of your glory.

33. Open the heavens O Lord, and turn my ridiculous to the miraculous.
34. Open the heavens O Lord, and turn my lack to great abundance.
35. Open the heavens O Lord, and broadcast yourself in every area of my life.
36. Send a rescue mission O Lord, to rescue me from the bondage of my father's house.
37. Send a rescue mission O Lord, to rescue from the pit of failure and discouragement.
38. Send a Rescue mission O Lord, to rescue me from the hand of every power enslaving me.
39. Send a rescue mission O Lord, to rescue me from the hands of ancestral problem refusing to let me go.
40. Let there be Open heavens and let my deliverance be made perfect.

MARKED FOR DESTRUCTION

Passages To Read Before You Pray:
- ❖ Pharaoh - Exodus 4:21; 6:1; 7:1-5; 14:4
- ❖ Ahab - 2 Chronicles 18:18 -34
- ❖ The Amalekites - Exodus 17: 8-16, 1 Sam 15: 1-35

PRAYER POINTS

1. I Seal myself and my household with the blood of Jesus from any attack of the enemy.
2. Every agent of confusion, assigned against my household today I mark you for destruction.
3. You agent of stagnancy assigned against my life, today you are marked for destruction.
4. You agent of failure assigned against my life, today you are marked for destruction.
5. Every serpentine spirit operating against my household, today you are marked for destruction.
6. Every serpentine spirit swallowing our prayers you are marked for destruction.
7. Every serpentine spirit assigned to rob me of my miracles, you are marked for destruction.
8. Every power that wants to make my problem permanent, you are marked for destruction.
9. Good things that the enemy thought they have completely destroyed in my life, Lord let there be restoration now.
10. Whatever needs to be done for me to receive my joy and miracles, Lord let it be done today.
11. Any power challenging God in my life, today you are marked for destruction.
12. Any power that wants me to remain in this situation, today, you are marked for destruction.

13. Any power working to hinder my progress, today you are marked for destruction.
14. Today by the power in the blood of Jesus, I am marked for favor.
15. Today by the power in the blood of Jesus, I am marked for progress.
16. Today by the power in the blood of Jesus, I am marked for success.
17. Today by the power in the blood of Jesus, I am marked for unusual breakthroughs
18. Today by the power in the blood of Jesus, I am marked for unbelievable miracles.
19. Today by the power in the blood of Jesus, I am marked for skyrocketing testimonies.
20. Today by the power in the blood of Jesus, I am marked for uncommon prosperity.

ON THE BASIS OF YOUR MERCY O LORD

Passages To Read Before You Pray:
Psalms 32; 51, Isaiah 64:4-9, Mark 10:46-52

PRAYER POINTS

1. Miracles that will give me a change of name, do it in my life O Lord.
2. Miracles that will give me a new and better story to tell, do it in my life O Lord.
3. Miracles that will change my status for the better do it in my life O Lord.
4. O God my Father, single me out for miracles.
5. O God my Father, single me out for prosperity
6. O God my Father, single me out for breakthrough.
7. O God my Father, single me out for promotion
8. O God my Father, let my cry attract divine intervention.
9. O God my Father, let my cry attract solution to every situation in my life.
10. On the basis of your mercy O Lord, hear my cry and attend to my case.
11. I refuse to get lost in the crowd, my cry must be heard.
12. I refuse to get lost in the crowd, I must receive solution.
13. I refuse to get lost in the crowd, I must receive my miracles.
14. I refuse to get lost in the crowd, the Lord will answer my prayer.
15. I refuse to get lost in the crowd, I must receive my healing.
16. On the basis of your mercy, heal me O Lord by your power.
17. On the basis of your mercy, bless me O Lord by your power.
18. On the basis of your mercy O Lord, I receive power to produce.

19. On the basis of your mercy O Lord, I receive power to prosper.
20. On the basis of your mercy O Lord, I receive power to flourish.
21. On the basis of your mercy O Lord, I claim anointing to function.
22. On the basis of your mercy O Lord, I claim restoration in every area of my life.
23. Every satanic crowd, trying to hinder my miracles I command you to scatter.
24. Every satanic crowd, trying to hinder my prayers I command you to scatter.
25. Every satanic crowd, trying to rob me of my breakthrough, I command you to scatter.
26. Every satanic crowd, trying to stand between me and my God, scatter in the name of Jesus Christ.
27. Today is my appointed time.
28. Today is my day of miracle.
29. Today is my healing day.
30. Touch me O Lord, so that I may be healed in the name of Jesus Christ.

DELIVERANCE FROM MISFORTUNE

Passages To Read Before You Pray:
Genesis 30:11, 1 Samuel 6:9, Ecclesiastes 9:11-12, Malachi 1:1-3

PRAYER POINTS

1. Father Lord, I thank you because you are the Most High God.
2. I reject misfortune in every area of my life in Jesus' name.
3. I reject misfortune in my business in the name of Jesus.
4. I reject misfortune in my marriage in the name of Jesus.
5. I reject misfortune in my relationship in the name of Jesus.
6. Spirit of misfortune, you will not hinder my prayers in the name of Jesus.
7. Spirit of misfortune, I cast you out of my life, I command you to leave and never come back in the name of Jesus.
8. Spirit of misfortune, you will not hinder my miracles.
9. Spirit of misfortune, you will not hinder my blessings
10. Spirit of misfortune, you will not hinder my progress.
11. Spirit of misfortune, you will not hinder my promotion.
12. Spirit of misfortune, you will not hinder my breakthrough.
13. Every seed of misfortune sown into my life, dry to your root and be consumed by fire.
14. Every seed of misfortune sown into my relationship, dry to your root and be consumed by fire.
15. Seed of misfortune affecting my business, come out with all your roots and be consumed by fire.
16. Seed of misfortune affecting my success, come out with all your roots and be consumed by fire.
17. Seed of misfortune affecting my progress, come out with all your roots and be destroyed by fire.

18. Seed of misfortune affecting my achievement, come out with all your roots and be destroyed by fire.
19. Seed of misfortune affecting my finances, come out with all your roots and be destroyed by fire.
20. Seed of misfortune affecting my children, come out with all your roots and be destroyed by fire.
21. Seed of misfortune driving my helpers away from me, come out with your roots and be destroyed by the fire of God.
22. O God my Father, set me free from the bondage of misfortune.
23. You spirit of misfortune, loose your hold over my life.
24. You spirit of misfortune, loose me and let me go in the name of Jesus.
25. Every bondage of misfortune, break in the name of Jesus.
26. Every yoke of misfortune, be destroyed by fire.
27. Anything in my life attracting misfortune to me, come out and be destroyed by fire.
28. I cancel every agreement that ties me to misfortune.
29. I break every curse of misfortune upon my life in the name of Jesus.
30. Every mark of misfortune upon my life be erased by the blood of Jesus.
31. Instead of misfortune, Father Lord, cover me with favor.
32. Instead of misfortune, Father let goodness and mercy follow me.
33. Instead of misfortune, Father Lord envelope me with your glory.

PRAYERS FOR PREGNANT WOMEN

Passages To Read Before You Pray:
Psalm 3; 9; 19; 23; 24; 27; 29; 46; 66; 91

PRAYER POINTS:

1. Father Lord, I thank you for giving me the gift of life.
2. O God my Father, I thank you for this wonderful blessing that is growing in my womb, may your name be praised for ever in the name of Jesus.
3. I hereby cover myself and my baby in the blood of Jesus Christ.
4. If there is anything in my blood that can negatively affect my baby, Father Lord, let it be neutralized by the blood of Jesus Christ.
5. O God my Father, let my baby continue to grow in your grace in the name of Jesus Christ.
6. O God my Father, let my baby receive the Holy Ghost right now even in the womb in the name of Jesus Christ.
7. O God my Father, make my time of pregnancy a smooth and wonderful experience, in the name of Jesus Christ.
8. I receive the grace and strength from God to carry my baby to full term in the name of Jesus Christ.
9. I reject any complication during and after my pregnancy in the name of Jesus Christ.
10. I shall not lose my baby in the name of Jesus Christ.
11. O God my Father, give my womb strength to hold my baby to full term in the name of Jesus Christ.
12. I reject premature birth in the name of Jesus Christ.
13. I claim wonderful and perfect baby, I reject any birth defect in the name of Jesus Christ.

14. O God my Father, grant my baby good health before and after birth in the name of Jesus Christ.
15. I reject down-syndrome or any birth defect on my baby in the name of Jesus Christ.
16. O God my Father, grant me good health during my pregnancy and after the birth of my baby in the name of Jesus Christ.
17. O God my Father, let every organ and part of my body work perfectly for normal development of my baby in the name of Jesus Christ.
18. I reject every satanic attack during my pregnancy in the name of Jesus Christ.
19. I reject sickness during my pregnancy, I shall be in good health in the name of Jesus Christ.
20. I refuse any curse in my bloodline to transfer into my baby in the name of Jesus Christ.
21. I refuse any ancestral problem to transfer into my baby in the name of Jesus Christ.
22. I refuse any ancestral sickness to transfer into my baby in the name of Jesus Christ.
23. Every evil blood covenant affecting me shall not affect my baby, I command you to break now in the name of Jesus Christ.
24. My baby shall be born to fulfill purpose and destiny in the name of Jesus Christ.
25. O God my Father, let anointing of ease rest upon me for the entire period of my pregnancy in the name of Jesus Christ.

PROMOTION

Passages To Read Before You Pray:
Genesis 45:8, 1 Samuel 2:7, 2 Samuel 7:8, 1Kings 14:7, Psalm 75,
Daniel 2:21

PRAYER POINTS

1. O God my Father, I thank you because you are my God; whoever you promote, no one can demote.
2. Anything that I have done against your will, that is hindering or delaying my promotion, Father forgive me
3. Cleans me O Lord, by the precious blood of Jesus.
4. It is high time O Lord; take me from where I am to where you want me to be.
5. Anything in my life delaying my promotion, get out of my life and be destroyed by fire.
6. Any mark of hatred upon my life affecting my promotion, be erased by the blood of Jesus.
7. Spirit of stagnancy fighting against me promotion, loose you hold upon my life,
8. Grant me favor O Lord, in the sight of those who will decide on my promotion.
9. Anyone that has the power and authority to promote me, you will not work against me in the name of Jesus.
10. Anyone that has the power and authority to promote me, whatever you do will work together for my good in the name of Jesus.
11. Anyone that has the power and authority to promote me, your decision will favor me in the name of Jesus.
12. I claim double promotion today, I reject demotion.
13. I claim double promotion today, I reject stagnation.

14. Every curse of demotion, break today by the power of God.
15. Any power fighting against my promotion, you will not prosper in the name of Jesus.
16. Any power delaying my promotion, you will not escape the judgment of God.
17. Any power postponing my promotion, you will not escape the judgment of God.
18. My promotion shall not be given to another man.
19. Father Lord, let those who have the power and the authority to promote me, remember me for good.
20. In my father's house, Lord, promote me and make me the head.
21. In my mother's house, Lord, promote me and make me the head.
22. Among my siblings, Lord, promote me and make me the head.
23. Among my friends, Lord, promote me and make me the head.
24. In my business, Lord, promote me and make me the head.
25. In my working place, Lord, promote me and make me the head.
26. O God my Father, let my promotion come now.
27. I reject every delay to my promotion in the name of Jesus.
28. My promotion that is given to another man, Father Lord, let it be restored back with me.
29. O God my Father, let everyone around me witness my promotion, so they may know that I serve a good God.
30. O God my Father, let people around me go extra mile to contribute to my promotion.
31. O God my Father, let every situation around me work together for my promotion.
32. I will be the head and not the tail in the name of Jesus.
33. O God my Father, convince my boss to promote me.

34. O God my Father, I am tired of being the same, take me to another level of promotion.
35. O God my Father, catapult me into greatness by your power.
36. O God my Father, catapult me to the top by your mighty hand.
37. Today, O Lord, remove every obstacle to my promotion.
38. Today, O Lord, remove every delay to my promotion.
39. Every spirit of doubt making me to lose my promotion, get out of my life and never come back.
40. O God my Father, let my promotion become a reality.
41. O God my Father, let your power promote me from poverty to riches.
42. O God my Father, let your power promote me from nobody to somebody.
43. O God my Father, let your power change my situation from the ridiculous to the miraculous.
44. O God my Father, promote me from where I am to sitting with kings and princes.
45. Father Lord, I thank you for answering my prayers.

SPIRITUAL GROWTH

Passages To Read Before You Pray:
Hebrews 6:1-3, John 15:1-27

PRAYER POINTS

1. O God my Father, open my understanding, I want to know more about you.
2. O God my Father, give me grace to bear fruits into the kingdom of heaven.
3. Holy Spirit of God, come and take your place in my heart and my life.
4. O God my Father, grant me grace to remain in you.
5. O God my Father, let your Word purify me and make me clean.
6. O God my Father, let the light of your Word illuminate my spirit.
7. Grace to obey you at all times, let it be granted unto me O Lord.
8. Father Lord, give me grace to study and follow your Word.
9. Anointing and grace to pray without ceasing let it rest upon me O Lord.
10. Anything in my life hindering my spiritual growth, Father Lord, remove it by your power.
11. Give me grace O Lord, to die to the flesh and be alive in the Spirit.
12. Let every work of the flesh in my life be replaced with the fruits of the Spirit.
13. O God my Father, let my life reflect your glory.
14. O God my Father, in your hands make me a vessel of honor.

SPIRITUAL HOUSE CLEANING

Passages To Read Before You Pray:
Genesis 35:1-5, Joshua 7:1-4, 24-26; 24:14, 23, 2 Samuel 21:1-14,
Acts 19:17-20

PRAYER POINTS

1. Any object (physical or spiritual) in my house attracting unseen guests, I break every covenant between you and me, and I set you on fire.
2. Any object in my house causing my life to go backward, I nullify every covenant between you and me, and I set you on fire.
3. Any object in my house causing my financial failure, I nullify every covenant between you and me and I set you on fire.
4. Any object in my house causing my life to be stagnated or putting my life on hold, I nullify every covenant between you and me, and I set you on fire.
5. Any objects in my house causing my business to fail or making me jobless, I nullify every covenant between you and me, and I set you on fire.
6. Any object in my house causing unexplainable sickness in the life of any member of my family, I nullify every covenant between you and my household, and I set you on fire.
7. Any object in my house causing me to live and swim in debts, I nullify every covenant between you and me, and I set you on fire.
8. Any objects in my house making sounds, movement and causing nightmares, I nullify every covenant between you and me, and I set you on fire.

9. Any object in my house attracting poverty to my household, I nullify every covenant between you and me, and I set you on fire.
10. Any object in my house attracting bad luck and misfortune to my household, I nullify every covenant between you and me, and I set you on fire.
11. Any object in my house that the enemy is using as a point of contact to carry out their mission, I nullify every covenant between you and me, and I set you on fire.
12. Any object in my house that enemies are using as entrance door to do evil, I nullify every covenant between you and me, and I set you on fire.
13. Every unholy thing in my house, from the top of the roof to the foundation, making my house a target to the enemy, I nullify every covenant between you and me, and I set you on fire.
14. Anything done by the past owners/residents/builder of my house, now affecting me, I destroy it and I terminate the bond between us.
15. Problems of the past owners/residents/builder of my house now manifesting in my life, I reject it and I nullify every covenant or bond between us.
16. Send your angels O Lord, to do a thorough search in my house and destroy every ungodly things that is affecting me.
17. Release your fire O Lord into my house to do total cleansing from every ungodly thing.
18. Open my eyes O Lord to recognize every ungodly thing in my house.
19. Anything in my house O Lord that you do not approve of, break all of them into irreparable pieces.
20. Every spirit and power that I have ignorantly permitted to invade my house, I command you to leave, you are no longer permitted.

21. Every spirit and power that the previous residents/owner or builder have permitted to invade my house, I command you to leave, you are no longer permitted.
22. Every spirit and power that have made my house their meeting place, I command you to leave, you are no longer permitted.
23. Every spirit and power sent to my house to frustrate me, I command you to leave, you are no longer permitted.
24. Every spirit and power sent to my house to oppress me, I command you to leave, you are no longer permitted.
25. I cover every nook and corner, every room and hallway in the blood of Jesus
26. Evil spirit that the past owners/residents/builder left behind in my house, I command you to leave, you are no longer permitted.
27. I seal up every spiritual door that leads in and out of my house by the blood of Jesus.
28. Every evil spirit that followed me home from any ungodly business that I have done, I repent and I command you to leave, you are no longer permitted.
29. Every evil spirit that I invited to my house through lying and cursing, I repent and I command you to leave, you are no longer permitted.
30. Every evil spirit that I invited to my house through TV shows, internet and video games, I repent and I command you to leave, you are no longer permitted.

WAR AGAINST MANIPULATING SPIRIT

Passages To Read Before You Pray:
Genesis 3:1-8, 2 Corinthians 2:11; 11:14, Matthew 4:1-11

PRAYER POINTS

1. Father Lord, I thank you for who you are in my life.
2. I cover myself and my household in the precious blood of Jesus
3. O God my Father, forgive me of all my past mistakes and iniquities.
4. Every manipulating spirit taking advantage of my mistakes, loose your hold over my life.
5. Every spirit manipulating me to disobey the law of God, you will not prosper over my life
6. Every spirit manipulating me to eat the forbidden fruit, you will not prosper over my life.
7. Every spirit manipulating me to work against myself, you will not prosper over my life.
8. Every spirit manipulating me in order to rob me of my glory, you will not prosper over my life.
9. Every spirit manipulating me in order to rob me of my joy, you will not prosper over my life.
10. Every spirit manipulating me in order to rob me of my miracles, you will not prosper over my life.
11. Every spirit manipulating me in order to rob me of my blessing, you will not prosper over my life.
12. Every spirit manipulating me in order to rob me of my breakthroughs, you will not prosper over my life.
13. Every spirit manipulating me in order to rob me of my success, you will not prosper over my life.

14. Every spirit manipulating me in order to rob me of my promotion, you will not prosper over my life.
15. Every spirit manipulating me in order to neutralize the power of God in me, you will not prosper over my life.
16. Every spirit manipulating me in order to corrupt my anointing, you will not prosper over my life.
17. Every spirit manipulating me to work against my own destiny, you will not prosper over my life.
18. Every spirit manipulating me to work against God's plan for my life, you will not prosper over my life.
19. Every spirit manipulating me to move out of my appointed location, you will not prosper over me.
20. Every spirit manipulating me in order to miss my open heaven, you will not prosper over my life.

REVIVE ME O LORD

Passages To Read Before You Pray:
Psalms 1; 19; 106, Isaiah 60:1-3; 61:1-1-3, Habakkuk 3:2

PRAYER POINTS:

1. O God my Father, strengthen me in any area that I am spiritually vulnerable.
2. Open my eyes O Lord, in any area that I am spiritually blind.
3. O God my Father, rekindle your fire in me
4. O God my Father, fill my heart with fire of revival.
5. If there is anything in my life that is affecting the growth of the body of Christ, Father, remove it now in the name of Jesus Christ.
6. O God my Father, give me grace to love others, even the unlovable and those that would not love me back.
7. Heal me O Lord, in any area that I am spiritually sick.
8. Help me O Lord, to recognize and acknowledge the importance of my fellow Christians to my spiritual growth.
9. In any area that my weakness is affecting the body of Christ, Father Lord, be my strength.
10. If there is any area that I am causing division in the body of Christ, Lord forgive me and correct me.
11. Spirit of pride that makes me to think more of myself, I rebuke you and cast you out of my life.
12. O God my Father, cloth me with humility.
13. O God my Father, let the fire of my love for you continue to burn and never go out.
14. Give me grace and anointing to build your kingdom not to tear it down.

ıT IS MY TIME TO FULFILL PURPOSE

Passages To Read Before You Pray:
Genesis 37:5-22, Jeremiah 32:17, Joel 2:21-24

PRAYER POINTS:

1. My destiny, bring out testimonies, in the name of Jesus.
2. Every dragon of my father's house pursuing my star, die, in the name of Jesus.
3. Every goat in the manger of my destiny, die, in the name of Jesus.
4. My star, refuse to be hidden, appear, in the name of Jesus.
5. Every journey into the palace of Herod, be cancelled in the name of Jesus.
6. Angels of the living God, possess my heavens for me in the name of Jesus.
7. Angels of the living God, arise and fill my dark night, in the name of Jesus.
8. Angels of the living God, arise, fight and recover my right places for me in the name of Jesus.
9. My Father, who reign upon the heavens of my life, arise and let the darkness in my heavens be disgraced in the name of Jesus.
10. Every restlessness in my days, hear me and hear me now, die, in the name of Jesus.
11. All powers and principalities in my heavens, be silenced by fire in the name of Jesus.
12. Anti-focus spirits, my life is not your candidate, scatter, in the name of Jesus.
13. My Father, if I have donated my virtues, I claim them back in the name of Jesus.
14. Every yoke of regret, break in the name of Jesus.
15. Every program of darkness to destroy my star, scatter in the name of Jesus.

16. Every power that must die for my breakthrough to manifest, die in the name of Jesus.
17. Every power that must be buried for my breakthroughs to manifest, I bury you by fire, in the name of Jesus.
18. O Lord, help me to be in the right place at the right time.
19. Every blessing that belongs to me but has gone back to heaven, come back in the name of Jesus.
20. Every power of my father's house pushing me away from my divine appointment, die in the name of Jesus.
21. O God! Arise and place me in my right location, in the name of Jesus.   .
22. Any power dragging me to where my angels of blessings will not locate me, die, in the name of Jesus.
23. Chariot of fire, clear away every blockage in my heavens, in the name of Jesus.
24. My Father, if I have been diverted from my land of promises, relocate me by fire, in the name of Jesus.
25. Everything done against me to spoil my joy in this year, be destroyed, in the name of Jesus.
26. I receive the goodness of the Lord in the land of the living, in the name of Jesus.
27. O Lord, as Abraham received favor in your hands, let me receive your favor so that I can excel, in the name of Jesus.
28. Lord Jesus, deal bountifully with me this year, in the name of Jesus.
29. It does not matter whether I deserve it or not, I receive unquantifiable favor from the Lord, in the name of Jesus.
30. Every blessing God has distributed to me in this year will not pass me by, in the name of Jesus.
31. My blessing will not be transferred to my neighbor, in the name of Jesus.
32. Father Lord, disgrace every power that are out to steal the blessings prepared for my life, in the name of Jesus.
33. Every step that I take this year shall lead to outstanding success, in the name of Jesus.
34. I shall prevail with man and with God, in the name of Jesus.

MY CHILDREN SHALL BE THE HEAD

Passages To Read Before You Pray:
Deuteronomy 28:1-14, Isaiah 8:18; 54:13

PRAYER POINTS:

1. O Lord, help my children to make prayer an important part of their lives, I pray in the name of Jesus Christ with much love and thanksgiving.

2. O God my Father, let excellent spirit rest upon and dwell in my children, I pray in the name of Jesus Christ with much love and thanksgiving.

3. I rebuke every vagabond spirit in the life of my children, I pray in the name of Jesus Christ with much love and thanksgiving.

4. Today, I cancel every demonic agenda against my children, I pray in the name of Jesus Christ with much love and thanksgiving.

5. Today, I cancel every plan of household wickedness against my children, I pray in the name of Jesus Christ with much love and thanksgiving.

6. Today, I destroy every negative spirit that is assigned against my children, I pray in the name of Jesus Christ with much love and thanksgiving.

7. As from today O Lord, surround my children with your mighty angels, I pray in the name of Jesus Christ with much love and thanksgiving.

8. No matter the plan of the enemy, my children shall fulfill their destiny, I pray in the name of Jesus Christ with much love and thanksgiving.

9. No matter the plan of the enemy, my children shall fulfill their God-given purpose, I pray in the name of Jesus Christ with much love and thanksgiving.

10. No matter the plan of the enemy, my children shall fulfill their dreams, I pray in the name of Jesus Christ with much love and thanksgiving.

11. Today, I decree success upon my children in whatsoever they do, I pray in the name of Jesus Christ with much love and thanksgiving.

12. Today, I decree breakthroughs into the life of my children, I pray in the name of Jesus Christ with much love and thanksgiving.

13. I rebuke any form of sickness in the life of my children, I pray in the name of Jesus Christ with much love and thanksgiving.

14. I decree divine protection upon my children, I pray in the name of Jesus Christ with much love and thanksgiving.

15. My children shall be the head and not the tail, I pray in the name of Jesus Christ with much love and thanksgiving.

16. Let the power of God neutralize every negative message that I have sent into the life of my children, I pray in the name of Jesus Christ with much love and thanksgiving.

17. Give my children grace O Lord, to know you more than I do, I pray in the name of Jesus Christ with much love and thanksgiving.

18. Give my children grace O Lord, to always have time for you, I pray in the name of Jesus Christ with much love and thanksgiving.

19. My children shall not be enticed away by the devil, I pray in the name of Jesus Christ with much love and thanksgiving.

20. My children shall not be what my enemies want them to be, I pray in the name of Jesus Christ with much love and thanksgiving.

21. Destiny destroyers will have no power over my children, I pray in the name of Jesus Christ with much love and thanksgiving.

22. Dream killers will have no power over my children, I pray in the name of Jesus Christ with much love and thanksgiving.

23. You violent spirit, I cast you out of my children's life, I pray in the name of Jesus Christ with much love and thanksgiving.

24. You lying spirit, I cast you out of my children's life, I pray in the name of Jesus Christ with much love and thanksgiving.

25. O God my Father, bestow your grace upon my children to overcome peer pressure, I pray in the name of Jesus Christ with much love and thanksgiving.

26. O God my Father, bestow your grace upon my children to make wise decision, even in the midst of chaos and storm, I pray in the name of Jesus Christ with much love and thanksgiving.

27. I command every evil flow in my family line to stop now, you can not affect my children, I pray in the name of Jesus Christ with much love and thanksgiving.

28. O God my Father, separate my children from evil associations, I pray in the name of Jesus Christ with much love and thanksgiving.

29. O God my Father, open my children's eyes to see and recognize the lies of the devil, I pray in the name of Jesus Christ with much love and thanksgiving.

30. Every cunningness of the devil shall fail over my children, I pray in the name of Jesus Christ with much love and thanksgiving.

31. The plan of the devil for the End times shall not affect my children, I pray in the name of Jesus Christ with much love and thanksgiving.

32. O God my Father, bestow your grace upon my children to overcome the danger of the End times, I pray in the name of Jesus Christ with much love and thanksgiving.

33. O God my Father, bestow your grace upon my children to stand against the wiles of the devil, I pray in the name of Jesus Christ with much love and thanksgiving.
34. O God my Father, bestow your grace upon my children to be spiritually sensitive, I pray in the name of Jesus Christ with much love and thanksgiving.
35. O God my Father, bestow your grace upon my children to recognize spirit of destruction when it comes, I pray in the name of Jesus Christ with much love and thanksgiving.
36. My children shall be for signs and wonders to the whole wide world, I pray in the name of Jesus Christ with much love and thanksgiving.
37. My children shall be like trees planted by the rivers of waters, I pray in the name of Jesus Christ with much love and thanksgiving.
38. O God my Father, give my children the spirit of power, boldness and sound mind, I pray in the name of Jesus Christ with much love and thanksgiving.
39. O God my Father, give my children divine wisdom and understanding like Solomon, I pray in the name of Jesus Christ with much love and thanksgiving.
40. Lord, let the Spirit of love dwell richly in the life of my children, I pray in the name of Jesus Christ with much love and thanksgiving.
41. O God my Father, bestow your grace upon my children to make you their Lord and Savior, I pray in the name of Jesus Christ with much love and thanksgiving.
42. Today, I break every generational curse in the life of my children, I pray in the name of Jesus Christ with much love and thanksgiving.
43. Today O Lord, deliver my children from evil spirit of this land, I pray in the name of Jesus Christ with much love and thanksgiving.

44. My mistake as parent shall not affect my children, I pray in the name of Jesus Christ with much love and thanksgiving.

DELIVERANCE FROM THE BONDAGE OF SPIRIT WIFE/HUSBAND

Passages To Read Before You Pray:
Psalms 56, 59, 60, 69, 70

PRAYER POINTS:

1. Every spirit wife/ husband, I do not love you, get out of my life and die, in the name of Jesus.
2. Everything you have deposited in my life, come out by fire, in the name of Jesus.
3. Every power working against my marriage, fall down and die, in the name of Jesus.
4. I divorce and renounce my marriage with the spirit husband/ wife, in the name of Jesus.
5. I break all covenants entered into with the spirit husband or wife, in the name of Jesus.
6. I command the thunder fire of God to burn to ashes the wedding gown, ring, photographs and all other materials used for the marriage, in Jesus' name.
7. I send the fire of God to burn to ashes the marriage certificate, in the name of Jesus.
8. I break every blood and soul-tie covenants with the spirit husband or wife, in the name of Jesus.
9. I send thunder fire of God to burn to ashes the children born to the marriage, in Jesus' name.
10. I withdraw my blood, sperm or any other part of my body deposited on the altar of the spirit husband or wife, in Jesus name.
11. You spirit husband or wife tormenting my life and earthly marriage, you are no longer allowed to do so, I bind you with hot chains and fetters of God and cast you out of my life into

the bottomless pit, and I command you not to ever come into my life again, in the name of Jesus.

12. I return to you, every property of yours in my possession in the spirit world, including the dowry and whatsoever was used for the marriage and covenants, in the name of Jesus.

13. I drain myself of all evil materials deposited in my body as a result of our sexual relation, in Jesus' name.

14. Lord, send Holy Ghost fire into my root and burn out all unclean things deposited in it by the spirit husband or wife, in the name of Jesus.

15. I break the head of the snake, deposited into my body by the spirit husband or wife to do me harm, and command it to come out, in the name of Jesus.

16. I purge out with the blood of Jesus, every evil material deposited in my womb to prevent me from having children on earth.

17. Lord, repair and restore every damage done to any part of my body and my earthly marriage by the spirit husband or wife, in the name of Jesus.

18. I reject and cancel every curse, evil pronouncement, spell, jinx, enchantment and incantation placed upon me by the spirit husband or wife, in the name of Jesus.

19. I take back and possess all my earthly belongings in the custody of the spirit husband or wife, in Jesus' name.

20. I command the spirit husband or wife to turn his or her back on me forever, in Jesus' name.

21. I renounce and reject the name given to me by the spirit husband or wife, in the name of Jesus.

22. I hereby declare and confess that the Lord Jesus Christ is my Husband for eternity, in Jesus' name.

23. I soak myself in the blood of Jesus and cancel the evil mark or writings placed on me, in Jesus' name.

24. I set myself free from the stronghold, domineering power and bondage of the spirit husband or wife, in the name of Jesus.
25. I paralyze the remote control power and work used to destabilize my earthly marriage and to hind me from bearing children for my earthly husband or wife, in the name of Jesus.
26. I announce to the heavens that I am forever married to Jesus.
27. Every trademark of evil marriage, be shaken out of my life, in the name of Jesus.
28. Every evil writing, engraved by iron pen, be wiped off by the blood of Jesus.
29. I bring the blood of Jesus upon the spirit that does not want to go, in the name of Jesus.
30. I bring the blood of Jesus on every evidence that can be tendered by wicked spirits against me.
31. I file a counter-report in the heavens against every evil marriage, in the name of Jesus.
32. I refuse to supply any evidence that the enemy may use against me, in the name of Jesus.
33. Let satanic exhibitions be destroyed by the blood of Jesus.
34. I declare to you spirit wife/ husband that there is no vacancy for you in my life, in the name of Jesus.
35. O Lord, make me a vehicle of deliverance.
36. I come by faith to mount Zion, Father Lord, command deliverance upon my life now.
37. Lord, water me from the waters of God.
38. Let the careful siege of the enemy be dismantled, in Jesus name
39. O Lord, defend your interest in my life.
40. Anything written against me in the cycle of the moon, be blotted out, in Jesus' name.
41. Anything programmed into the sun, moon and stars against me, be dismantled, in Jesus' name.

42. Every evil thing programmed into my genes, be blotted out by the blood of Jesus.
43. O Lord, shake out seasons of failure and frustrations from my life.
44. I overthrow every wicked law working against my life, in the name of Jesus.
45. I ordain a new time, season and profitable law, in Jesus' name.
46. I speak destruction unto the palaces of the queen of the coast and of the rivers, in Jesus' name.
47. I speak destruction unto the headquarters of the spirit of Egypt and blow up their altars, in the name of Jesus.
48. I speak destruction unto the altars, speaking against the purpose of God for my life, in Jesus' name.
49. I declare myself a virgin for the Lord, in Jesus' name.
50. Let every evil veil upon my life be torn open, in Jesus' name.
51. Every wall between me and the visitation of God, be broken, in the name of Jesus.
52. Let the counsel of God prosper in my life, in the name of Jesus.
53. I destroy the power of any demonic seed in my life from the womb, in the name of Jesus.
54. I speak unto my umbilical gate to over throw all negative parental spirits, in the name of Jesus.
55. I break the yoke of the spirit, having access to my reproductive gates, in the name of Jesus.
56. O Lord, let your time of refreshing come upon me.
57. I bring fire from the altar of the Lord upon every evil marriage, in the name of Jesus.
58. I redeem myself by the blood of Jesus from every sex trap, in the name of Jesus.
59. I erase the engraving of my name on any evil marriage record, in the name of Jesus'.

60. I reject and renounce every evil spiritual marriage, in the name of Jesus.
61. I confess that Jesus is my original spouse and is jealous over me.
62. I issue a bill of divorcement to every spirit wife/ husband, in the name of Jesus.
63. I bind ever spirit wife/ husband with everlasting chains, in the name of Jesus.
64. Let heavenly testimony overcome every evil testimony of hell, in the name of Jesus.
65. O Lord, bring to my remembrance every spiritual trap and contract.
66. Let the blood of Jesus purge me of every contaminating material, in the name of Jesus.
67. Let the spirit husband/wife fall down and die, in Jesus name.
68. Let all your children attached to me fall down and die, in the name of Jesus.
69. I burn your certificates and destroy your rings, in Jesus name.
70. I execute judgment against water spirits and declare that you are reserved for everlasting chains in darkness, in Jesus name.
71. O Lord, contend with those who are contending with me.
72. Every trademark of water spirit, be shaken out of my life, in the name of Jesus.
73. Spirit husband/spirit wife, release me by fire, in Jesus name.
74. Every spirit husband/ wife, I divorce you by the blood of Jesus.

I AM GETTING MY LIFE BACK

Passages To Read Before You Pray:
Psalms 3, 9, 35, 55, 68, 140

PRAYER POINTS:

1. Stubborn bewitchment, what are you waiting for? Die in Jesus' name.
2. Every witchcraft giant of poverty, die today, in the name of Jesus.
3. Thou power of marriage destruction, die in the name of Jesus.
4. Every arrow of witchcraft, fired into my dream, backfire, today in the name of Jesus.
5. Every arrow of infirmity and untimely death, go back to your sender in the name of Jesus.
6. Every cage of witchcraft, release my star in the name of Jesus.
7. O Lord! Ordain terrifying noise against the enemies of my breakthrough in the name of Jesus.
8. O God that answers by fire, answer my request and I shall glorify your name.
9. Oh thou that trouble my Israel, my God shall trouble you today in the name of Jesus.
10. Every robber of my destiny, die in the name of Jesus.
11. I command my spirit to drop every bag with a hole, in Jesus' name.
12. Holy Ghost and fire, possess my possessions for me, in the name of Jesus.
13. Every foundational power working against my complete deliverance, die in Jesus' name.

14. Every power of my father's house contesting for my deliverance, die in the name of Jesus.
15. Every power of my family line, arguing with my angel of breakthroughs, die in the name of Jesus.
16. Every arrow of the enemy fired into my head, backfire, in the name of Jesus.
17. O God, be God in my situation in the name of Jesus.
18. Every barrier on my way to breakthroughs, die in the name of Jesus.
19. Holy Ghost fire, bulldoze my way to breakthroughs in the name of Jesus.
20. Inherited Red Sea blocking my ways to the promise land, divide in the name of Jesus.
21. Every spiritual barrier hanging over my head, scatter in the name of Jesus.

PRAYERS FOR CHURCH

Passages To Read Before You Pray:
Psalms 79, 80, Matthew 16:18

PRAYER POINTS:

1. I destroy the clock and the timetable of the enemy for this church, in Jesus name.
2. Let every evil device against this church be disappointed.
3. O Lord, wake up every member of this church from any form of spiritual sleep.
4. Let your kingdom and your will be established in every area of this ministry.
5. Every arrow of failure and destruction fired at this church, go back to sender.
6. O Lord, let the tongues of the enemy of growth of this church be divided and confused.
7. Let all the counsels of the wicked break.
8. In this church, O Lord, give us a miracle that will dumbfound the whole world.
9. Father Lord, let us experience victory in every area of this ministry.
10. I bind every activity and operation of the devil in this environment.
11. Let every evil association against this ministry be severely destabilized.
12. Fire of God, minister destruction to the ministry of destruction in every area of this ministry.
13. Let all the enemies of our progress start their days with confusion and end it in destruction.

14. O Lord God Almighty, speak life into every area of this ministry.
15. Father Lord, speak growth into every area of this ministry.
16. Father Lord, open the inner eyes of every member of this church to see what you have called them to be.
17. In the name of Jesus, I command this church to spread, to the south, north, east, and west.
18. Lord, bring new members from every part of the world, from every tongue, tribe, language, and color.
19. Father Lord, rebuild every department of this church into perfection.
20. Remember your promises, O Lord, fulfill them now, enemies are mocking.

I REFUSE TO BE POOR

Passages To Read Before You Pray:
Deuteronomy 30:9, Psalm 115: 12-18, Isaiah 30:23; 60:1-22

PRAYER POINTS:

1. O heavens over my prosperity, open by fire in the name of Jesus
2. Angels of poverty, clear from the gate of my breakthroughs in the name of Jesus.
3. O wealth, jump out of the prison of the wicked and locate me now in the name of Jesus.
4. You children of darkness continue to labor, at the end of your labor transfer the wealth to me in the name of Jesus.
5. I eat the sweat of my enemies by the power in the blood of Jesus in the name of Jesus.
6. Angels of the living God, pursue wealth into my hands in the name of Jesus.
7. Any power that wants me to die as a pauper, you are a liar, die in the name of Jesus.
8. I withdraw my wealth from the hand of the bondwoman and her children, in the name of Jesus.
9. I will not squander my divine opportunities, in the name of Jesus.
10. I dismantle any power working against my efficiency, in the name of Jesus.
11. I refuse to lock the door of blessings against myself, in the name of Jesus.
12. I refuse to be a wandering star, in the name of Jesus.
13. I refuse to appear to disappear, in the name of Jesus.

14. Let the riches of the Gentiles be transferred to me, in the name of Jesus.
15. Let the angels of the Lord pursue every enemy of my prosperity to destruction, in the name of Jesus.
16. Let the sword of the Goliath of poverty turn against it, in the name of Jesus.
17. Let wealth replace poverty in my life, in the name of Jesus.
18. Lord, make a hole in the roof for me for my prosperity.
19. Let the yoke of poverty upon my life be dashed to pieces, in the name of Jesus.
20. Let every satanic siren scaring away my helpers be silenced now, in the name of Jesus.
21. Let every masquerading power swallowing my prosperity be destroyed, in the name of Jesus.
22. Let every coffin constructed against my prosperity swallow the owner, in the name of Jesus.
23. Let the ways of the angels of poverty delegated against me be dark and slippery, in the name of Jesus.
24. Lord Jesus, touch and bless my purse.
25. Every demonic scarcity, be dissolved by fire, in the name of Jesus.
26. By the wealthy name of Jesus, let heavenly resources rush to my door.
27. I attack my lack with the sword of fire, in the name of Jesus.
28. Satanic debt and credit, be dissolved, in the name of Jesus.
29. O Lord, be my eternal cashier.
30. I bind the spirit of debt. I shall not borrow to eat, in the name of Jesus.
31. Every evil meeting summoned against my prosperity, scatter without repair, in the name of Jesus.
32. Every arrow of wickedness, fired against my prosperity, be disgraced, in the name of Jesus.

33. Let my life magnetize favor for breakthroughs, in the name of Jesus.
34. I arrest every gadget of poverty, in the name of Jesus.
35. I recover my blessings from any body of water, forest and satanic banks, in the name of Jesus.
36. Let all my departed glory be restored, in the name of Jesus.
37. Let all my departed virtues be restored, in the name of Jesus.
38. Let God arise and let all my stubborn pursuers scatter, in the name of Jesus.
39. Every attack by evil night creatures, be disgraced, in the name of Jesus.
40. Let the wings of every spirit flying against me be dashed to pieces, in the name of Jesus.
41. Angels of the living God, search the land of the living and the land of the dead and recover my stolen properties, in the name of Jesus.
42. Every gadget of frustration, be dashed to pieces, in the name of Jesus.
43. I break every curse of poverty working upon my life, in the name of Jesus.
44. I bind every spirit drinking the blood of my prosperity, in the name of Jesus.
45. Lord, create new and profitable opportunities for me.
46. Let ministering angels bring customers and favor to me, in the name of Jesus.
47. Anyone occupying my seat of prosperity, be removed by fire, in the name of Jesus.
48. Lord, make a way for me in the land of the living.
49. I bind the spirit of fake and useless investment, in the name of Jesus.
50. All unsold materials, be sold with profit, in the name of Jesus.
51. Let all business failure be converted to success, in the name of Jesus.

52. Every curse on my hands and legs, be broken, in the name of Jesus.
53. Lord, bless me with abundance in every area of my life.
54. Every strange money affecting my prosperity, be neutralized, in the name of Jesus.
55. Let brassy heavens break forth and bring rain, in the name of Jesus.
56. I break the control of every spirit of poverty over my life, in the name of Jesus.
57. Lord Jesus, anoint my eyes to see the hidden riches of this world.
58. Lord Jesus, advertise Your breakthroughs in my life.
59. Let the riches of the ungodly be transferred into my hands, in the name of Jesus.
60. I will rise above the unbelievers around me, in the name of Jesus.
61. Lord, make me a reference point of divine blessings.
62. Let blessings invade my life, in the name of Jesus.
63. Let the anointing of excellence fall on me, in the name of Jesus.
64. I disarm satan's power and authority over my prosperity, in the name of Jesus.
65. Let harvest meet harvest in my life, in the name of Jesus.
66. Let harvest overtake the sower in my life, in the name of Jesus.
67. Every curse pronounced against my source of income, be broken, in the name of Jesus.
68. Let my breakthroughs turn around for good, in the name of Jesus.
69. Curses working against my destiny, break, in the name of Jesus.
70. Lord, network me with divine helpers.

71. Let life-transforming breakthroughs overtake me, in the name of Jesus.
72. Let divine ability overtake me, in the name of Jesus.
73. Lord, lead me to those who will bless me.
74. Let my favor frustrate the plan of the enemy, in the name of Jesus.
75. I will witness the downfalls of my strongman, in the name of Jesus.
76. I will be a lender and not a borrower, in the name of Jesus.
77. My labor shall not be in vain, in the name of Jesus.
78. Let the blessings which there will be no room to receive overtake me, in the name of Jesus.
79. Lord, plant me by the rivers of prosperity.
80. Unknown evil seeds in my life, I command you to refuse to germinate, in the name of Jesus.
81. I refuse to get stuck on one level of blessing, in the name of Jesus.
82. I shall possess all the good things I pursue, in the name of Jesus.
83. Every effect of cursed house and land upon my prosperity, break, in the name of Jesus.
84. Every power shielding me away from breakthroughs, fall down and die, in the name of Jesus.
85. Let the garden of my life yield super abundance, in the name of Jesus.
86. Every desert spirit, loose hold upon my life, in the name of Jesus.
87. Holy Spirit, plug my life into divine prosperity, in the name of Jesus.
88. Every Achan in the camp of my breakthroughs, be exposed and be disgraced, in the name of Jesus.
89. Every power operating demonic gadget against my prosperity, fall down and die, in the name of Jesus.

90. Every power passing evil current into my finances, lose your hold, in the name of Jesus.
91. I break every cycle of financial turbulence, in the name of Jesus.
92. I smash the head of poverty, walk out of my life now, in the name of Jesus.
93. Ugly feet of poverty, walk out of my life now, in the name of Jesus.
94. Let every garment of poverty received the fire of God, in the name of Jesus.
95. I reject financial burial, in the name of Jesus.
96. Let every garment of poverty received the fire of God, in the name of Jesus.
97. I reject financial burial, in the name of Jesus.
98. I reject every witchcraft burial, in the name of Jesus.
99. Woe unto every vessel of poverty pursuing me, in the name of Jesus.

PART 2

1. Let the fire of God burn away evil spiritual properties, in the name of Jesus.
2. Poverty-identification marks, be rubbed off by the blood of Jesus.
3. Lord, heal every financial leprosy in my life.
4. Let my foundation be strengthened to carry divine prosperity, in the name of Jesus.
5. Every stolen and satanically transferred virtues, be restored, in the name of Jesus.
6. Let every ordination of debt over my life be canceled, in the name of Jesus.
7. Lord, create newer and profitable opportunities for me.

8. Every strange fire ignited against my prosperity, be quenched, in the name of Jesus.

9. Let those sending my money to spiritual mortuary fall down and die, in the name of Jesus.

10. Every power scaring away my prosperity, be paralyzed, in the name of Jesus.

11. Every familiar spirit sharing my money before I received it, be bound permanently, in the name of Jesus.

12. Let every inherited design of poverty melt away by fire, in the name of Jesus.

13. Let every evil re-arrangement of prosperity be dismantled, in the name of Jesus.

14. Lead me, O Lord, to my own land that flows with milk and honey.

15. Let satanic giants occupying my promised land fall down and die, in the name of Jesus.

16. Lord, empower me to climb my mountain of prosperity.

17. Strongman of poverty in my life, fall down and die, in the name of Jesus.

18. Spirits of famine and hunger, my life is not your candidate, in the name of Jesus.

19. I remove my name from the book of financial embarrassment, in the name of Jesus.

20. Every power reinforcing poverty against me, loose your hold, in the name of Jesus.

21. I release myself from every bondage of poverty, in the name of Jesus.

22. The riches of the gentiles shall come to me, in the name of Jesus.

23. Let divine magnet of prosperity be planted in my hands, in the name of Jesus.

24. I retrieve my purse from the hand of Judas, in the name of Jesus.

25. Let there be a reverse transfer of my satanically transferred wealth, in the name of Jesus.
26. I take over the wealth of the sinner, in the name of Jesus.
27. I recover the steering wheels of my wealth from the hand of evil drivers, in the name of Jesus.
28. I refuse to lock the door of blessings against myself, in the name of Jesus.
29. Lord, revive my blessings.
30. Lord, return my stolen blessings.
31. Lord, send God's angels to bring me blessings.
32. Lord, let everything that needs change in my life to bring me blessings be changed.
33. Lord, uncover to me my key for prosperity.
34. Every power sitting on my wealth, fall down and die, in the name of Jesus.
35. Lord, transfer the wealth of Laban to my Jacob.
36. Let all those who hate my prosperity be put to shame, in the name of Jesus.
37. Every evil bird swallowing my money, fall down and die, in the name of Jesus.
38. Every arrow of poverty, go back to where you came from, in the name of Jesus.
39. I bind every word spoken against my breakthroughs, in the name of Jesus.
40. Every business house energized by satan, fold up, in the name of Jesus.
41. I destroy every clock and timetable of poverty, in the name of Jesus.
42. Every water spirit, touch not my prosperity, in the name of Jesus.
43. Let men and women rush wealth to my doors, in the name of Jesus.
44. I reject temporary blessings, in the name of Jesus.

45. Every arrow of poverty energized by polygamy, fall down and die, in the name of Jesus.
46. Every arrow of poverty energized by household wickedness, fall down and die, in the name of Jesus.
47. Let there be a positive and dramatic turnaround in my finances, in the name of Jesus.
48. Let every serpent and scorpion of poverty die, in the name of Jesus.
49. I refuse to eat the bread of sorrow. I reject the water of affliction, in the name of Jesus.
50. Let divine explosion fall upon my breakthroughs, in the name of Jesus.
51. The enemy will not drag my finances on the ground, in the name of Jesus.
52. Lord, advertise your wealth and power in my life, in the name of Jesus.
53. Let promotion meet promotion in my life, in the name of Jesus.
54. I pursue and overtake my enemies and recover my wealth from them, in the name of Jesus.
55. Holy Spirit, direct my hands into prosperity, in the name of Jesus.
56. Begin to thank God for answers to your prayers.

ARISE AND DISGRACE YOUR ENEMIES

Passages To Read Before You Pray:
Psalms 2, 3, 18, 27, 55

PRAYER POINTS:

1. Lord, empower my prayer altar by fire.
2. Lord, soak me in the spirit of prayer.
3. Let God arise in His anger and fight for me.
4. I refuse to allow my angels of blessings to depart, in Jesus' name.
5. I cancel every evil effect of names from evil origins in my life, in the name of Jesus.
6. I paralyze all aggression addressed at my star, in Jesus' name.
7. I neutralize all problems originating from the mistakes of my parents, in the name of Jesus.
8. Lord, bring honey out of the rock for me.
9. Lord, open up all the good doors of my life that household wickedness has shut.
10. Let all anti-breakthrough designs against my life be shattered to irreparable pieces, in the name of Jesus.
11. I paralyze all satanic antagonism from the womb, in Jesus' name.
12. I command open disgrace on the mask of the enemy, in Jesus' name.
13. I paralyze all evil legs roaming about for my sake, in Jesus' name.
14. Let all evil blood that has mingled with my blood be drained out, in the name of Jesus.
15. I trample upon every enemy of my advancement and promotion, in the name of Jesus.
16. I break every evil collective unity organized against me, in the name of Jesus.

17. Let all evil counselors against me follow the wrong program, in the name of Jesus.
18. Let the backbone of the stubborn pursuer and strongman break, in the name of Jesus.
19. I destabilize the controller of any land of bondage in my life, in the name of Jesus.
20. Lord, enlarge my coasts beyond my wildest dream.
21. Holy Ghost, seal all pockets that have demonic holes, in Jesus' name.
22. Let the fire of disgrace fall upon demonic prophets assigned against my life, in the name of Jesus.
23. No evil meeting held on my behalf shall prosper, in Jesus' name.
24. I claim back my goods presently residing in wrong hands, in the name of Jesus.
25. Let the blood and strength of stubborn oppressors dry up, in the name of Jesus.
26. Let the head of every serpent power fashioned against me be broken, in the name of Jesus.

I RECEIVE POWER TO MOVE FORWARD

Passages To Read Before You Pray:
Psalms 1, 57, 68, 94, Isaiah 60:1-22

PRAYER POINTS:

1. I reject the life that floats like a dead fish, in the name of Jesus.
2. I reject every spirit of the tail and I claim the spirit of the head, in the name of Jesus.
3. Every inherited failure in my life, die in the name of Jesus.
4. I will reach my goal, whether the devil likes it or not, in the name of Jesus.
5. Every environmental influence caging my life, break in the name of Jesus.
6. I shall not surrender to my enemies it is my problem that shall surrender, in the name of Jesus.
7. I shall not be in the wrong profession, in the name of Jesus.
8. O God of promotion! Promote my life by fire, in the name of Jesus.
9. I shall not come to the world in vain, in the name of Jesus.
10. My enemies shall not use my time in vain, in the name of Jesus.
11. O wealth of the Gentiles, locate me, in the name of Jesus.
12. O Lord, open my eyes, in the name of Jesus.
13. Holy Spirit, be my partner, in the name of Jesus.
14. I decree civil war into the camp of my hardened enemies, in the name of Jesus.
15. I command my life to move from minimum to maximum, in the name of Jesus.
16. Every power harassing my life, I disgrace you today, in the name of Jesus.
17. Every poison of witchcraft, come out of my destiny, in the name of Jesus.

18. Every Pharaoh from the waters pursuing my life, die, in the name of Jesus.
19. Every satanic supreme court working against me, die in the name of Jesus.
20. Every witchcraft altar in my family, your time is up, die, in the name of Jesus.
21. Every stumbling block on my way to breakthroughs, I kick you out, in the name of Jesus.
22. O Lord, I hate your enemies with perfect hatred, in the name of Jesus.
23. Every marine stronghold in my family, break in the name of Jesus.
24. I break the power of every incense lit against me, in the name of Jesus.
25. Every battle against my destiny, from my foundations, die in the name of Jesus.
26. Every architect of afflictions, from my foundations, scatter, in the name of Jesus.
27. Stones of fire locate foundational Goliath, in the name of Jesus.
28. Every foundational strong man, causing problems for my life, die, in the name of Jesus.
29. Every familiar spirit stealing my virtue, scatter in the name of Jesus.
30. Every strange power gathered against my advancement, die, in the name of Jesus.
31. Every satanic power planning my disgrace, die in the name of Jesus.
32. Every satanic panel set up against me, scatter in the name of Jesus.
33. Every bird of darkness holding vigil, your time is up, die, in the name of Jesus.
34. O God my Father, change my present speed to divine speed, in the name of Jesus.
35. Every ancestral wall built around my glory, die, in the name of Jesus.
36. My glory under bondage, receive deliverance by fire, in the name of Jesus.

37. My helpers in captivity, come out, in the name of Jesus.
38. By fire by thunder, O God, arise and disgrace my confusions, in the name of Jesus.
39. Every witchcraft agent of my father's house, die, in the name of Jesus.
40. My opportunities in bondage, come out, in the name of Jesus.
41. O God my Father, visit me today, in the name of Jesus.
42. Every clock and time-table working against me must be buried, in the name of Jesus.
43. The enemy will not drag my life on the ground, in the name of Jesus.
44. O God my Father, show me your ways, in the name of Jesus.
45. Angels of breakthroughs, encamp around me, in the name of Jesus.
46. Let power of signs and wonders overshadow my life, in the name of Jesus.
47. Every agenda of the wasters for my life, die, in the name of Jesus.
48. My blood, reject the arrow of death, in the name of Jesus.
49. My virtues, depart from the valley of the enemies, in the name of Jesus.
50. You power of marine witchcraft, die, in the name of Jesus.
51. Every darkness in my life, your time is up, die, in the name of Jesus.
52. O camp of my enemies, receive confusion, in the name of Jesus.
53. Every arrow of sickness and untimely death, backfire, in the name of Jesus.
54. Holy Ghost fire, arise in your anger, bury my Goliath, in the name of Jesus.
55. Every poison programmed into my body, die, in the name of Jesus.
56. Every unrepentant enemy of my progress, scatter, in the name of Jesus.
57. O God! You are mighty in battle, pursue my pursuers, in the name of Jesus.
58. Every local river abhorring my blessings, release them by fire, in the name of Jesus.

59. O Lion of Judah, roar into the camp of my enemies, in the name of Jesus.
60. I pull down every stronghold of poverty, in the name of Jesus.
61. O God arise, promote me into your power house, in the name of Jesus.
62. O God, arise and surprise my enemies, in the name of Jesus.
63. My Father! By the thunder of your power, arrest my arresters, in the name of Jesus.
64. Every owner of evil loads, hear the word of the Lord, carry your load by fire, in the name of Jesus.
65. Every priest of darkness working against my destiny, I retrench you, in the name of Jesus.
66. Every arrow of charms, fired against my destiny, backfire, in the name of Jesus.
67. Every ritual power working against my destiny, die, in the name of Jesus.
68. O heavens, disgrace my oppressors, in the name of Jesus.
69. Every witchcraft embargo on my destiny, be removed and be destroyed, in the name of Jesus.
70. My virtue that is in the custody of witchcraft, arise and come out, in the name of Jesus.
71. Satanic time-table for my life, die, in the name of Jesus.
72. Let every root of hardship, die, in the name of Jesus.
73. Let every arrow fired into my brain backfire, in the name of Jesus.
74. Let every enemy of my ancestors that are working against my destiny, die, in the name of Jesus.
75. Let every power that summons my spirit man in the night, die, in the name of Jesus.
76. O God my Father, let my life shine forth your glory, in the name of Jesus.

RECEIVING POWER TO PROSPER

Passages To Read Before You Pray:
Deuteronomy 8:18, Joshua 1:8, Psalm 115:12-18

PRAYER POINTS:

1. O Heaven of my prosperity, open by fire, in the name of Jesus.
2. O God, arise and empower me to prosper, in the name of Jesus.
3. Every power seating on my wealth, fall down and die, in the name of Jesus.
4. Foundational poverty, die, in the name of Jesus.
5. I take authority and I bind the strongman over my financial failure, in the name of Jesus.
6. I break every covenant of poverty of my father's house, in the name of Jesus.
7. I enter into the covenant of prosperity and abundance with the El shaddai, in the name of Jesus.
8. Every curse and covenant responsible for financial mess, I revoke you, in the name of Jesus.
9. Every power that will contend with my divine destiny this year, scatter, in the name of Jesus.
10. O star of my destiny, arise and shine this year, in the name of Jesus.
11. I silence every strange altar sacrificing my divine opportunities, in the name of Jesus.
12. Blood of Jesus, wipe off all handwriting of failure in my life.
13. Every tree of misfortune, be uprooted from my life by fire, in the name of Jesus.

14. Fire of God, deal with every root of misfortune, in the name of Jesus.
15. When and where others are confused, I shall succeed, I shall get maximum profit, in the name of Jesus.
16. O God, arise and teach me how to make profit, in the name of Jesus.
17. O God, arise and teach me how to produce wealth, even in a bad economy, in the name of Jesus.
18. My Father, breathe upon all I will do this year, in the name of Jesus.
19. Every strongman of failure at the edge of my breakthroughs, die, in the name of Jesus.
20. Blood of Jesus, dissolve the root of disgrace, in the name of Jesus.
21. Every ancestral debt-collector forcing me to pay what I do not owe, die, in the name of Jesus.
22. I reject the life of survival on debt. I receive financial breakthroughs to clear the debts, in the name of Jesus.
23. Every power of family curse and covenant of poverty over my life, break, in the name of Jesus.
24. Those that despise me in the past shall see my favor, in the name of Jesus.
25. Those who belittle me shall witness my progress, in the name of Jesus.
26. Every cycle of backwardness, break, in the name of Jesus.
27. Prosperity famine, die, in the name of Jesus.
28. Every seed of failure planted in my family line, die, in the name of Jesus.
29. Every power of aimlessness, die, in the name of Jesus.
30. I ask for the release of prosperity on my life, in the name of Jesus.
31. Let all demonic hindrances to my finances be totally paralyzed, in the name of Jesus.

32. Fire of God, destroy all demonic bags holding my breakthroughs, in the name of Jesus.
33. Every power in my foundation, waging war against my destiny, die, in the name of Jesus.
34. Let men go out of their ways to show favor unto me, in the name of Jesus.
35. Lord, let not the lot of the wicked fall upon my life, in the name of Jesus.
36. Every satanic investigation into my future, be dismantled, in the name of Jesus.
37. O Lord, give me the achievements that will swallow up my past failure, in the name of Jesus.
38. Every weapon of shame directed against my life, loose your power, in the name of Jesus.
39. Every satanic arrow fired at my star, fall down and die, in the name of Jesus.
40. My destiny, jump out of debt, in the name of Jesus.
41. Every enemy of my progress, scatter, in the name of Jesus.
42. Every enemy of my miracles, scatter, in the name of Jesus.
43. O Lord, shake down the foundation of hardship in my life, in the name of Jesus.
44. Every blessing that has passed me by, return, in the name of Jesus.
45. Fire of God, melt away every handwriting of poverty, in the name of Jesus.

I SHALL RECOVER ALL

Passages To Read Before You Pray:
1 Samuel 30, Psalms 18, 126, Joel 2:25-27

PRAYER POINTS:

1. Thank God for His love, and mercy on you.
2. Praise the Lord with all your heart for what He is about to do in your life.
3. God my Father, ordain terrifying noises unto the camp of the enemies of the gospel in my life (II Kings 7:6, 7).
4. I command every satanic embargo on my goodness and prosperity to be scattered to irreparable pieces, in the name of Jesus.
5. Let every door of attack on my spiritual progress be closed, in Jesus' name.
6. Holy Spirit, set me on Fire for God.
7. I command all my imprisoned benefits to be released, in Jesus' name.
8. God my Father, anoint me to pull down negative strongholds standing against me, in the name of Jesus.
9. Let the thunder fire of God strike down all demonic strongholds manufactured against me.
10. God my Father, anoint me with the power to pursue, overtake and recover my stolen properties from the enemy.
11. God my Father, bring to naught every evil counselor and his counsel against me.
12. The enemy shall not have a hiding place in my life in Jesus' name.
13. Let all blocked ways of prosperity be open up in Jesus' name.

14. I command the devil to take his legs off my finances in Jesus' name.
15. I paralyze every spirit of Goliath with the stones of fire in the name of Jesus.
16. I command every demonic transport vehicle loading away my benefits to be paralyzed, in the name of Jesus.
17. I receive the power to pursue every stubborn pursuer into the red sea, in the name of Jesus.
18. Let the mandate issued to every robber of my blessing be rendered null and void, in the name of Jesus.
19. Father Lord, send someone like Moses to face my Pharaoh and someone like David to face my Goliath.
20. Let the wheels of all pursuing evil chariots be shattered, in the name of Jesus.
21. I pursue and overtake all forces of household wickedness and I recover my stolen items from them, in the name of Jesus.
22. Let blessings, goodness and prosperity pursue and overtake me, in the mighty name of Jesus.
23. I command all my properties captured by spiritual robbers in the dream to become too hot to handle and to come back to me, in the name of Jesus.

I SPEAK RESTORATION

Passages To Read Before You Pray:
1 Samuel 30, Psalms 18, 126, Joel 2:25-27

PRAYER POINTS:

1. Let there be light in every area of my life that I have lost ground to the power of darkness.
2. I get my life back from the hand of evil controller.
3. Lord, speak restoration into every area of my spiritual life.
4. Lord, speak restoration into every area of my natural life.
5. Lord, speak restoration into every area of my finances.
6. Lord, speak restoration into the life of every member of my family.
7. Lord, speak restoration into every area of my business.
8. Lord, speak restoration into every area of my interest.
9. Lord, speak restoration into every area that I have lost hope in my life.
10. Dry bones in every area of my spiritual life, I command you, rise and live again.
11. Dry bones in every area of my natural life, I command you, rise and live again.
12. Dry bones in every area of my finances, I command you, rise and live again.
13. Dry bones in every area of my marriage I command you, rise and live again.
14. Dry bones in the life of every member of my family, I command you, rise and live again.
15. Dry bones in every area of my business, I command you, rise and live again.

I SPEAK SOLUTION

Passages To Read Before You Pray:
Jeremiah 32:17, Luke 1:37; 9:1, John 11:40-44

PRAYER POINTS:

1. Spirit and power of infirmity, I command you in the name of Jesus, loose your hold over my life.
2. Spirit and power of failure, loose me and let me go.
3. Spirit and power of stagnancy, loose me and let me go.
4. Spirit and power of almost there, loose me and let me go.
5. Spirit and power of the tail, loose me and let me go.
6. Spirit and power of backwardness, loose me and let me go.
7. Spirit and power of slavery, loose me and let me go.
8. Spirit and power of hard labor, loose me and let me go
9. Spirit and power of fruitlessness, loose me and let me go.
10. Spirit and power of every negative word spoken against my life, loose me and let me go.
11. Spirit and power of demotion, loose me and let me go.
12. Spirit and power of misfortune, loose me and let me go.
13. Spirit and power of poverty, loose me and let me go.
14. O my life, receive divine touch from the Lord.
15. O my situations, receive divine touch from the Lord.
16. Every part of my body, receive the healing touch from the Lord.
17. O my spiritual life, receive divine touch from the Lord.
18. O my material life, receive divine touch from the Lord.
19. O my finances, receive divine touch from the Lord.
20. O my destiny, receive divine touch from the Lord.
21. O my business, receive divine touch from the Lord.

22. O my life, I command you in the name of Jesus, be productive.
23. O my life, I command you in the name of Jesus, excel.
24. O my life, I command you in the name of Jesus, be promoted.
25. With authority and power, I speak favor into my life.
26. With authority and power, I speak breakthrough into my life.
27. With authority and power, I speak solution to my situations.
28. With authority and power, I speak healing to every part of my body.
29. With authority and power, I speak hope to my hopeless situation.
30. With authority and power, I speak divine provision to all my needs.
31. With authority and power, I speak greatness into my life.
32. With authority and power, I speak help to my helpless situation.
33. With authority and power, I break every yoke of stagnancy.
34. With authority and power, I break every yoke of failure.
35. With authority and power, I break every curse placed on my life.
36. With authority and power, I break every yoke of poverty.
37. With authority and power, I break every yoke of fruitless hard work.
38. With authority and power, I break every yoke of fruitless efforts.
39. With authority and power, I break every yoke of loneliness.
40. With authority and power, I break every yoke of bad luck.

FATHER, DEPOSIT YOUR WONDERS

Passages To Read Before You Pray:
Psalms 30, 35, 46, Joel 2:21, Habakkuk 1:5,

PRAYER POINTS:

1. I challenge my spiritual battle by the fire of the Holy Ghost.
2. I challenge and destroy every satanic operation against my life.
3. O Lord, anoint me for favor.
4. I bind every prince of the air that is hindering my progress.
5. I break the covenants that strengthen my enemy, in Jesus name.
6. I declare every spiritual slavery broken.
7. I cancel every legal claim of my enemy over my life.
8. O Lord, take me from where I am to where you want me to be.
9. Every word spoken against me by my enemies shall not stand.
10. I pull down every barrier to my greatness.
11. I receive divine wings to fly into my high places.
12. O Lord, set me ablaze with your Spirit.
13. Lord Jesus, destroy every satanic foundation and build me upon your divine foundation.
14. Holy Spirit, deposit your wonders in my life by fire.
15. Every enemy of my breakthroughs, I exercise dominion over you.
16. I refuse to appear consciously or unconsciously by any evil summon.
17. The yoke of evil spirit shall not reign over my visions.

18. O God, re-arrange my life breakthroughs.
19. I dismantle spiritual devices working against my destiny.
20. I overthrow and cancel every council of wickedness against my life.
21. Lord, help me to hear your voice and to make right decisions in my life all the time.
22. O Lord, empower me to become the person you created me to be.
23. Every stagnation and failure, receive fire of God and be destroyed.
24. I shall fulfill my divine purpose, nothing shall dethrone me, in Jesus name.
25. I command and release my divine helpers to manifest, in Jesus name.
26. O Lord, arise and sit over my life and let my destiny change for the better.
27. My promotion shall not be taken away from me.
28. Every pattern of slavery, break, in Jesus name.
29. I withdraw the comfort of any strongman working against me, in Jesus name.
30. I raise a standard against every spirit fighting against my efforts, in Jesus name.
31. O Lord, start what the world cannot stop in my life.
32. Every ministry of killing, stealing and destruction working against me receive the fire of God and die.
33. Anointing that brings miracles, fall on me.
34. Anointing for constant open heavens, fall on me.
35. Every satanic investment in my life, be wasted.
36. Satanic agenda for my life, vanish, in Jesus name.
37. Every blessing that comes into my hand shall never fall off, in Jesus name.
38. Every enemy that has refused to let me go, receive double destruction.

39. I enter into my prophetic destiny, in Jesus name.

I DECREE SUCCESS

Passages To Read Before You Pray:
Job 22:28, Psalms 59, 69, 70, Isaiah 54:17

PRAYER POINTS:

1. Deliver me O Lord, from the bondage of vision destroyers.
2. Deliver me O Lord, from the cage of my household enemies.
3. Deliver me O lord, from the bondage and power of destiny changers.
4. I cover my destiny with the blood of Jesus.
5. O my destiny, reject evil, in the name of Jesus.
6. O my destiny, reject every demonic attack.
7. Every conspiracy against my destiny, scatter by fire.
8. Every evil mouth speaking against my destiny, I condemn you, in the name of Jesus.
9. I condemn every power fighting against my destiny.
10. I condemn every power fighting against my future.
11. I condemn every power fighting against my success.
12. I condemn every power standing against my breakthroughs.
13. I condemn every power standing against my miracles.
14. I condemn every power standing against my testimonies
15. Every power that wanted me to pray in vain, I condemn you.
16. Every power that wanted me to labor in vain, I condemn you.
17. Every power that wanted me to work for nothing, I condemn you.
18. Every power renewing my solved problems, I condemn you.
19. Every mouth speaking failure into my life, I condemn you.
20. Every mouth speaking backwardness into my life, I condemn you.
21. Every mouth speaking evil into my finances, I condemn you.

22. Every mouth that is speaking evil into my marriage, I condemn you.
23. O my life, it is time for you to get better, in the name of Jesus.
24. Father Lord, heal my foundation.
25. Father Lord, heal my finances.
26. Father Lord, heal my house/marriage.
27. Hear me O heaven, I decree my success in the name of Jesus.
28. Hear me O heaven, I decree my promotion in the name of Jesus.
29. Hear me O heaven, I decree my breakthroughs in the name of Jesus.
30. Hear me O heaven, I decree my miracles in the name of Jesus.
31. Hear me O heaven, I decree my ways open right now.
32. O my heavens of prosperity, I declare you open, in the name of Jesus.
33. I refuse to do according to the will of my enemies.
34. I refuse to follow the road map or my enemies
35. O my heavens of abundance, I declare you open.
36. O my heavens of surplus, I declare you open.
37. O my heavens of testimonies, I declare you open.
38. O my heavens of breakthroughs, I declare you open.
39. O my heavens of signs and wonders, I declare you open.
40. My time of promotion, come now by fire.
41. My time of breakthroughs, come now by fire.

I CLAIM FINANCIAL BREAKTHROUGHS

Passages To Read Before You Pray:
Deuteronomy 8:18, Joshua 1:8, Psalm 115:12-18

PRAYER POINTS:

1. Any curse upon my life turning my blessings away from me, break now in the name of Jesus.
2. Any curse upon my life, scattering all my blessings, break, in the name of Jesus.
3. O my Angel of spiritual blessings, locate me by fire.
4. O my Angel of material blessings, locate me by fire.
5. O my Angel of financial blessings, locate me by fire.
6. O my Angel of prosperity, locate me by fire.
7. I refuse to work for someone else to eat.
8. Open my eyes O Lord, to the source of my financial breakthroughs.
9. Order my footsteps O Lord, and lead me to the source of my financial blessings.
10. Order my footsteps O Lord, and lead me to the source or my material blessings.
11. Order my footsteps O Lord, and lead me to the source or my spiritual blessings.
12. Money shall not run away from me in the name of Jesus.
13. Let anointing to make money in easy ways without stress fall upon me.
14. Your word says, All things are mine, I claim my financial breakthroughs.
15. Your word says, All things are mine, I claim my spiritual blessings.
16. I claim my material blessings.

17. Father Lord, give me some divine money yielding ideas that will change my life forever.
18. Tell me what to do O Lord, to tap into the money you put in treasury for me, and show me how to do it.
19. Divine advice that will lead to my financial breakthrough, I receive it in Jesus name.
20. Information that will lead me to my financial freedom, I receive it in Jesus name.
21. Every curse that will not allow me to listen to my financial freedom advice, break now.
22. I claim my financial freedom today.
23. I reject financial embarrassment.
24. Every man and woman that has information of my financial freedom, I command you to locate me by fire.
25. Every man and woman that has information of my breakthroughs, I command you, locate me by fire.

HEAR MY CRY, O LORD

Passages To Read Before You Pray:
Psalms 61, 64, 67, 74, 83

PRAYER POINTS:

1. Lord, I thank you for opening my eyes of understanding to realize that I need some prayers.
2. Lord, why is my life the way it is? My life needs to be fixed, fix my life today for your name's sake.
3. Have I done anything to attract failure? I bow to my knee, Lord have mercy on me.
4. O God my Father, break every curse that had vowed to forever delay or hinder my miracles.
5. Release upon me O Lord, uncommon grace to overcome all my challengers and to put them to shame.
6. Remove from me O Lord, any spirit focusing on what I see in my environment than what you have designed for me.
7. In the name of Jesus, I rebuke every spirit in me and around me that vowed to never let me succeed.
8. In the name of Jesus, I bind and cast out every spirit in me and around me that vowed to never let me breakthrough.
9. In the name of Jesus, I bind and cast out every spirit in me and around me that vowed to only let me work hard like a slave but would have nothing to show.
10. In the name of Jesus, I bind and cast out every spirit in me and around me that has been hindering my prayers.
11. In the name of Jesus, I bind and cast out every spirit in me and around me that has been delaying my miracles.
12. In the name of Jesus, I bind and cast out every spirit in me and around me that has been making my life miserable.

13. In the name of Jesus, I cast down every mountain of problems in my life, and I command you to never rise again.
14. In the name of Jesus, I cast down every evil imagination against me making my life hell on earth.
15. I know there is no problem that is greater than you, O Lord, let my problems vanish, so I can start a new and fulfilling life.
16. Lord, I need a miracle that would change my life positively forever.
17. Lord, I need a sudden miracle that would happen before my enemies suspect anything.
18. Lord, I need a miracle that will turn my mourning to dancing.
19. Lord, I need a miracle that will turn my ridicules to testimonies.
20. Lord, I need a miracle that would be very hard to believe for anyone.
21. Lord, I need a miracle that will put me above my contemporaries.
22. Lord, I need a miracle that will change my status in every area of life.
23. O God my Father, roll away from my life, every reproach of my father's house.

ACCELERATE MY PROGRESS

Passages To Read Before You Pray:
Psalms 2, 23, 30, 103, 126

PRAYER POINTS:

1. Thank God for what He has done for you this year.
2. Let frustration and disappointment, be the portion of every object fashioned against my life and family, in the name of Jesus.
3. Every evil tie to polluted objects and items between my life and family, break, in the name of Jesus.
4. Every unspoken curse against my life, break, in the name of Jesus.
5. Every curse pronounced inwardly against my destiny, break, in the name of Jesus.
6. You inward curses, fighting against my virtues, break, in the name of Jesus.
7. Any power, given the mandate to curse and hinder my progress, be rendered useless and die, in the name of Jesus.
8. Let every spirit of Balaam hired to curse my progress, fall down and die, in the name of Jesus.
9. Every curse that I have brought into my life through ignorance and disobedience, break by fire, in the name of Jesus.
10. Every power magnetizing physical and spiritual curses to me, I raise the blood of Jesus against you and I challenge you by fire, in the name of Jesus.
11. Father, Lord, turn all my self-imposed curses to blessings, in the name of Jesus.

12. Every instrument put in place to frustrate me become impotent, in the name of Jesus.
13. I reject every cycle of frustration, in the name of Jesus.
14. Every agent assigned to frustrate me, perish by fire, in the name of Jesus.
15. Every power tormenting me, die by the sword, in the name of Jesus.
16. I destroy the power of every satanic arrest in my life, in the name of Jesus.
17. All satanic-arresting agents, release me in the mighty name of our Lord Jesus Christ.
18. Anything representing me in the demonic world against my career, be destroyed by the fire of God, in the name of Jesus.
19. Spirit of the living God, quicken the whole of my being, in the name of Jesus.
20. God, smash me and renew my strength, in the name of Jesus.
21. Holy Spirit, open my eyes to see beyond the visible to the invisible, in the name of Jesus.
22. Lord, ignite my career with Your fire.
23. O Lord, liberate my spirit to follow the leading of the Holy Spirit.
24. Holy Spirit, teach me to pray through problems instead of praying about, it in the name of Jesus.
25. O Lord, deliver me from the lies I tell myself.
26. Every evil spiritual padlock and evil chain hindering my success, be roasted, in the name of Jesus.
27. I rebuke every spirit of spiritual deafness and blindness in my life, in the name of Jesus.
28. O Lord, empower me to resist satan that he would flee.
29. I chose to believe the report of the Lord and no other, in the name of Jesus.
30. Lord, anoint my eyes and my ears that they may see and hear wondrous things from heaven.

31. O Lord, anoint me to pray without ceasing.
32. In the name of Jesus, I capture every power behind any career failure.
33. Holy Spirit, rain on me now, in the name of Jesus.
34. Holy Spirit, uncover my darkest secrets, in the name of Jesus.
35. You spirit of confusion, loose your hold over my life, in the name of Jesus.
36. In the power of the Holy Spirit, I defy satan's power upon my career, in the name of Jesus.
37. Let water of life flush out every unwanted stranger in my life, in the name of Jesus.
38. You the enemies of my career, be paralyzed, in the name of Jesus.
39. O Lord, begin to clean away from my life all that does not reflect You.
40. Holy Spirit fire, ignite me to the glory of God, in the name of Jesus.
41. O Lord, let the anointing of the Holy Spirit break every yoke of backwardness in my life.
42. I frustrate every demonic arrest over my spirit-man, in the name of Jesus.
43. Let the blood of Jesus remove any unprogressive label from every aspect of my life, in Jesus' name.
44. Anti-breakthrough decrees, be revoked, in the name of Jesus.
45. Holy Ghost fire, destroy every satanic garments in my life, in the name of Jesus.

THE BEST IN ME, COME FORTH

Passages To Read Before You Pray:
Deuteronomy 28:1-14, Isaiah 54:1-17; 60:1-22

PRAYER POINTS:

1. Father Lord, I can see the hands of the enemy all over my life, I cannot go on like this, do something now.
2. Lord, this is not how you created me, look down and deliver me from the hands of the power recreating my life.
3. O God my Father, bring out the best that you have deposited in me.
4. Every garment of the enemy that covers the best in me, I set you on fire and I command the best in me to shine forth.
5. Every demonic covering over the glory of God in me, disappear now, in Jesus name.
6. I receive anointing to do better than this lifestyle, in the name of Jesus.
7. I know I can live a better life, I command the best in me to shine forth.
8. I know I can have a better future, I command the best in me to shine forth.
9. I know I can get a better job, I command the best in me to shine forth.
10. I know I can handle my breakthrough, I command the best in me to produce great things.
11. I know I can handle my breakthrough, I command the best in me to yield better results.
12. I know I can handle my breakthrough, I command the best in me to bring out divine ideas that will reveal me to the world.

13. I know I can handle my promotion, I command the best in me to come out by fire.
14. Father Lord, let the people that will help me begin to see the best that you have deposited in me.
15. Father Lord, help me to live a better life because you have deposited the best in my life.
16. The best in me that is dying, come alive by fire.
17. The best in me that is rusty, receive the life of God and shine.
18. I refuse to exchange the best of God in me with failure.
19. I refuse to exchange the best of God in me with demotion.
20. I refuse to exchange the best of God in me with backwardness.
21. I refuse to exchange the best of God in me with sickness.
22. I refuse to exchange the best of God in me with misfortune.
23. I refuse to exchange the best of God in me with misfortune.
24. I receive divine strength and anointing to bring out the best of God in me.
25. I receive grace to recognize the best of God in me.
26. I shall not produce less than the best of God in me
27. I shall not use the best of God in me to make others great.
28. The best of God in me shall make me great.
29. The best of God in me shall make me the head and a great leader.

IT IS MY TIME TO SHINE

Passages To Read Before You Pray:
Job 22:28, Proverbs 18:21, Isaiah 60:1-22,

PRAYER POINTS:

1. It is my time to shine, I command every curse of stagnancy to break in Jesus name.
2. It is my time to shine, I command every curse of failure to break.
3. It is my time to shine, I command every curse of debt to break.
4. It is my time to shine, I command every curse of backwardness to break.
5. It is my time to shine, I command every curse of sickness to break.
6. It is my time to shine, I command every curse of emptiness to break.
7. It is my time to shine, I command every curse of almost there to break.
8. It is my time to shine, I command every curse of poverty to break.
9. It is my time to shine, I command every curse of nakedness to break.
10. It is my time to shine, I command every curse of last minute denial to break.
11. Every opposition against my breakthroughs, be cancelled, in Jesus' name.
12. Every opposition against my success, be cancelled, in Jesus' name.

13. Every conspiracy to hold me down at the bottom of the ladder, scatter, in Jesus name.
14. Every conspiracy of the enemy to keep me in bondage, scatter.
15. I refuse to settle for the offer of the enemies.
16. I break every curse holding me back from fulfilling my destiny.
17. I break every curse delaying my success.
18. Every curse upon my life delaying my promotion, break.
19. Every curse upon my life delaying my breakthrough, break.
20. Every curse upon my life that has determined to make me a loser, break now.
21. I break every agreement that I have made to destroy my life.
22. I terminate every contract signed by anyone to make me a slave.
23. It is my time to shine, I command the best of God in me to manifest by fire.
24. It is my time to shine, I command all my dreams to come alive.
25. Father Lord, let the greatness that you have put in me come out by fire and prove my enemies wrong.
26. Father Lord, let the best in me shine forth and put my enemies to shame.
27. I receive special anointing today to achieve my goals.
28. I receive special anointing today to fulfill my dreams.
29. Father Lord, let your mighty hands rest upon me today and bring the best out of me.
30. Father Lord, set my finances free today from the hands of my enemies.
31. Let my divine helpers see the best of God in me.
32. My enemies shall bow before my star like the case of Joseph.
33. I refuse to cooperate with the plan of the enemy against my life.

34. I cancel and destroy every demonic agenda against my life.
35. Every mouth speaking evil against me shall not prosper in Jesus name.
36. I refuse to cooperate with the plan of the enemy to make me a beggar.
37. I refuse to cooperate with the plan of the enemy to make me a failure.
38. I refuse to cooperate with the plan of the enemy to make me a loser.
39. I refuse to cooperate with the plan of the enemy to make me homeless.
40. I refuse to cooperate with the plan of the enemy to make me poor.
41. I receive anointing and power to receive and manage my blessings.
42. I receive anointing and power to get and control wealth.
43. I receive anointing and power to receive and keep my breakthroughs.
44. Today shall mark the beginning of my success.
45. Today shall mark the beginning of my breakthroughs.
46. I command the best of God in me to produce greatness.
47. I command the best of God in me to make ways for me.
48. I command every area of my life to be productive.
49. Today shall mark the beginning of my greatness.
50. I shall not lack any good thing.
51. I shall live to fulfill my purpose.
52. I shall live to enjoy the fruits of my labor.
53. Every evil handwriting against me shall not stand, be erased by the blood of Jesus.

I REFUSE TO COOPERATE

Passages To Read Before You Pray:
Psalms 3, 34, 35, 94, 106

PRAYER POINTS:

1. I refuse to cooperate with the power that wants to destroy my life.
2. I refuse to cooperate with the power that wants to destroy my future.
3. I refuse to cooperate with the power that wants to destroy my vision.
4. I refuse to cooperate with the power that wants to destroy my dream.
5. I refuse to cooperate with the power that wants to destroy my finances.
6. I refuse to cooperate with the power that wants to rob me of my blessings.
7. I refuse to cooperate with the power that is holding me captive.
8. I refuse to cooperate with the power that wants to destroy my destiny.
9. I refuse to cooperate with the plan of the enemies to change my destiny.
10. I refuse to cooperate with the power of the enemies fighting against my prayer.
11. Father Lord, let the plan of the enemy fail over my life.
12. Father Lord, let the plan of the enemy fail over my household.
13. Father Lord, let the plan of the enemy fail over my future.
14. Father Lord, let the plan of the enemy fail over my finances.

15. Father Lord, let the plan of the enemy fail over my destiny.
16. Every evil arrow shot at me by the enemy, go back to sender.
17. Every arrow of sudden death shot at me by the enemy, go back to sender.
18. Every arrow of sudden destruction shot at me by the enemy, go back to your sender.
19. Every arrow of sickness shot at me by the enemy, go back to sender.
20. Every arrow of failure shot at me by the enemy, go back to sender.
21. Father Lord, let your angel of destruction go through the camp of my enemies.
22. The expectation of the enemy over my life shall not stand.
23. The expectation of the enemy over my job/business shall not stand.
24. The expectation of the enemy over my ministry shall not stand.
25. The expectation of the enemy over my future shall not stand.
26. The expectation of the enemy over my dream shall not stand.
27. The expectation of the enemy over my purpose in life shall not stand.
28. The expectation of the enemy over my finances shall not stand.
29. The expectation of the enemy over my household shall not stand.
30. I shall laugh last over the enemy of my soul.
31. I shall laugh last over the enemy of my progress.
32. I shall laugh last over the enemy of my promotion.
33. I shall laugh last over the enemy of my success.
34. I shall laugh last over the enemy of my breakthroughs.
35. I shall laugh last over the enemy of my life.
36. I shall laugh last over the enemy of my dreams.
37. I shall laugh last over the enemy of my vision.

38. Enemy that refuses to give up on my life shall die before his time.
39. Enemy that refuses to give up on my breakthrough, die before your time.
40. I receive anointing to overcome every problem of life.
41. I receive anointing to overcome every financial problem in my life.
42. Father Lord, take away the power of boasters boasting over my life.
43. Father Lord, take away the power of boasters boasting over my success.
44. Father Lord, take away the power of boasters boasting over my household.
45. Father Lord, take away the power of boasters boasting over my breakthroughs.
46. Father Lord, take away the power of boasters boasting over my achievements.
47. Father Lord, take away the power of boasters boasting over my future.
48. I refuse to quit and I command my enemies to surrender.
49. I refuse to quit and I command my blessings to manifest by fire.
50. I refuse to quit and I command my helpers to locate me by fire.
51. I refuse to quit and I command my breakthroughs to come by fire.
52. I refuse to quit and I command my promotion to come by fire.
53. I refuse to quit and I command my stars to shine by fire.

DELIVERANCE FROM THE POWER OF "NO"

Passages To Read Before You Pray:
Psalms 35, 59, 69, 70, Isaiah 54:17

PRAYER POINTS:

1. I condemn every tongue saying NO to my breakthroughs.
2. I condemn every tongue saying NO to my success.
3. I condemn every tongue saying NO to my prosperity.
4. I condemn every tongue saying NO to my good health.
5. I condemn every tongue saying NO to all my blessings.
6. I condemn every tongue saying NO to my miracles.
7. I condemn every tongue saying NO to my peace of mind.
8. I condemn every tongue saying NO to my progress.
9. I condemn every tongue saying NO to my prayers.
10. I condemn every tongue saying NO to my promotions.
11. I condemn every tongue saying NO to the YES of God in my life.
12. I condemn every tongue saying NO to my spiritual growth.
13. I condemn every tongue saying NO to my dream & vision.
14. I condemn every tongue saying NO to my freedom.
15. I command my blessings to be released from captivity.
16. I command my breakthrough to be released from captivity.
17. I command my life to be released from captivity.
18. I command my entire household to be released from captivity.
19. I command my promotion to be released from captivity.
20. I command my finances to be released from captivity.
21. I command every member of my church family to be released from captivity.
22. I command my miracles to be released from captivity.

23. I command my success to be released from captivity.
24. I command the answers to all my prayers to be released from captivity.
25. Deliver me O God, from the hands of my enemies.
26. Deliver me O God, from the hands of my household wickedness.
27. Deliver me O God, from the hands of destiny changers.
28. Deliver me O God, from the hands of the enemies of my soul.
29. Deliver me O God, from the hands of the enemies of my progress.
30. Deliver me O God, from the hands of my pharaoh.
31. Deliver me O God, from the hands of my taskmaster.
32. Deliver me O God, from the hands of the enemies of my breakthroughs.
33. Deliver me O God, from the hands of the power that wants me dead.
34. Deliver me O God, from the hands of the enemies of my prosperity.
35. Deliver me O God, from the hands of the power that wants to destroy my home.
36. Deliver me O God, from the hands of the power that wants to take away my joy.
37. Deliver me O God, from the hands of the power that wants to take away my peace.
38. Deliver me O God, from the hands of the power robbing me of my miracles.
39. Deliver me O God, from the hands of the power robbing me of my blessings.
40. Deliver me O God, from the hands of the power attacking me with sickness.
41. Deliver me O God, from the hands of the enemy of my promotion.

42. Deliver me O God, from the hands of the enemy attacking my future.
43. Deliver me O God, from the hands of the wicked and their wickedness.
44. Deliver me O God, from the hands of the enemy that wants to destroy my dream.
45. Deliver me O God, from the hands of the enemy trying to enslave me.
46. Deliver me O God, from the bondage of poverty.
47. Deliver me O God, from the bondage of stagnancy.
48. Deliver me O God, from the hands of my unrepentant enemies.
49. Every evil pronouncement over my life, be cancelled, in Jesus name.
50. Every evil pronouncement over my household, be cancelled.
51. Every evil pronouncement over my future, be cancelled.
52. Every evil pronouncement over my destiny, be cancelled.
53. Every evil pronouncement over my finances, be cancelled.
54. Every evil pronouncement over my glory, be cancelled.
55. Every evil pronouncement over my dreams, be cancelled.
56. Every evil pronouncement over my church, be cancelled.

ENOUGH IS ENOUGH

Passages To Read Before You Pray:
Psalms 30, 83, 109, Joel 2:21-24, Habakkuk 1:5

PRAYER POINTS:

1. Father Lord I have suffered enough from the hands of my enemies, let my days of joy come.
2. Father Lord I have suffered enough from the hands of my household wickedness, let my glory appear by fire.
3. Father Lord I have suffered enough from the hands of the spirit of poverty, let my blessings come right now.
4. Father Lord I have suffered enough from the hands of the spirit of stagnancy, let my life move forward.
5. Father Lord I have suffered enough delay, let my life progress.
6. Father Lord I have suffered enough demotion, let my promotion come by fire.
7. Father Lord I have suffered enough from the hands of sickness, let my healing be made perfect.
8. Father Lord I have suffered enough slavery, liberate me by fire.
9. Father Lord I have suffered enough chains and bondage, set me free today.
10. Father Lord I have suffered enough failure, from this moment I shall fail no more.
11. Father Lord I have suffered enough disappointment, from this moment surround me with good people.
12. Father Lord I have suffered enough shame, remove my shame today by your power.
13. Father Lord I have suffered enough pain, heal my pain now.

14. My days of joy shall come by fire.
15. My time of prosperity, come by fire.
16. My hour of deliverance, come now by fire.
17. My days of blessings, come now by fire.
18. My days of miracles, come now by fire.
19. Blood of Jesus, wipe away every mark of poverty.
20. Blood of Jesus, wipe away every mark of sickness.
21. Blood of Jesus, wipe away every mark of sudden death.
22. Blood of Jesus, wipe away every mark of backwardness.
23. Blood of Jesus, wipe away every mark of failure.
24. Blood of Jesus, wipe away every mark of the enemy.
25. Blood of Jesus, wipe away every mark of failure at the edge of miracles.
26. O God my Father, put an end to my pain.
27. O God my Father, put an end to my sickness.
28. O God my Father, put an end to my sorrow.
29. O God my Father, put an end to my failure.
30. O God my Father, put an end to hard labor less blessings in my life.
31. O God my Father, put an end to my crying.
32. O God my Father, put an end to my hopeless situations.
33. O God my Father, put an end to poverty in my life.
34. O God my Father, put an end to sufferings in my life.

TAKING CONTROL OF YOUR NEIGHBORHOOD

Passages To Read Before You Pray:
Isaiah 47:1-15, Ephesians 1:17-23; 6:10-18

PRAYER POINTS:

1. I cover myself in the blood of Jesus.
2. O God my Father, forgive me of anything that I have done, that gave access to the enemies to torment me.
3. I receive the grace of God and I forgive everyone that have offended me.
4. O God my Father, let the blood of Jesus cleanse me and make me whole.
5. Territorial power in my neighborhood, causing my life to be stagnated, I bind you and cast you into hell.
6. Territorial spirit in my neighborhood, causing my life to go backward, I bind you and cast you into hell.
7. Evil power in my neighborhood setting limits on people's progress, I am not your candidate, I bind you and cast you into hell.
8. Evil power in my neighborhood delaying my progress, lose your hold over my life, I blind you and cast you into hell.
9. Evil power in my neighborhood inflicting people with different kinds of sickness and disease, I am not your candidate, I bind you and cast you into hell.
10. Evil power in my neighborhood placing embargo on people's life, I am not your candidate, lose your hold over my life.
11. Spirit of poverty ruling over my neighborhood, I am not your candidate, lose your hold over my life.

12. Territorial spirit over my neighborhood inflicting people with untimely death, I am not your candidate, lose your hold over my life.
13. Evil power in my neighborhood causing businesses to fail and making people jobless, I am not your candidate.
14. Dispatch your angels O Lord, to sweep my neighborhood.
15. Send your fire O Lord, to destroy every territorial power in my neighborhood.
16. Dispatch the hosts of heaven O Lord, to fight and eliminate territorial power in my neighborhood.
17. I Charge the atmosphere in my neighborhood by the fire of God and make it unbearable for territorial power.
18. I declare my neighborhood holy unto the Lord.
19. Covenants between territorial powers and anyone in my neighborhood is hereby nullified by the fire of God.
20. Territorial Spirit, you are no longer permitted to terrorize my neighborhood.
21. Territorial spirit, you are no longer allowed to control the affairs of my neighborhood.
22. Territorial spirit, you are no longer allowed to dwell in my neighborhood.
23. Today, my neighborhood is delivered from the bondage of territorial spirit and power.
24. Anything or anyone in my neighborhood attracting evil to us, get out now and be destroyed.
25. Anything or anyone attracting bad luck and misfortune to my neighborhood, be destroyed by the fire of God.
26. Anything un-holy that makes my neighborhood a target to the enemy, I set you on fire.
27. Anything or anyone attracting poverty and lack to my neighborhood, be destroyed by the fire of God.

28. Anything done by the past owners, resident and builders of my neighborhood now affecting me, be destroyed by fire of God.

29. Dispatch your angels O Lord, to do thorough search in my neighborhood and destroy every work of territorial power.

30. Because I live in this neighborhood, territorial spirit and power are not allowed.

31. Territorial spirit and power, lose your hold over my neighborhood.

32. Territorial spirit and power, you are no longer allowed to affect our success in this neighborhood.

33. Territorial spirit and power, you are no longer allowed to hinder my prayers.

34. Territorial spirit and power, you are no longer allowed to delay my miracles.

35. Territorial spirit and power, you are no longer allowed to tamper with my destiny.

36. Territorial spirit and power, you are no longer allowed to kill our dreams.

37. O God arise, fight and destroy every agent of darkness in my neighborhood.

38. Territorial spirit and power, I am no longer under your bondage.

39. Let the light of God overcome the darkness in my neighborhood.

40. Let the Spirit of love and unity be established in my neighborhood.

41. O God my Father, let success become standard in my neighborhood.

42. O God my Father, let promotion become common thing in my neighborhood.

43. In my neighborhood O Lord, deliver every marriage from the hands of territorial spirit and power.

44. In my neighborhood O Lord, deliver our children from the hands of territorial spirit and power.
45. Today O Lord, deliver our businesses from the hands of territorial spirit and power.
46. O God my Father, let prosperity be released into my neighborhood.
47. O God my Father, establish your kingdom in my neighborhood.
48. O God my Father, deliver my finances from the hands of territorial spirit and power.
49. I seal every spiritual door that leads in and out of my neighborhood by the blood of Jesus.
50. Spirits of oppression and depression in my neighborhood, I command you to leave, you are no longer allowed to operate.

PRAYERS OF THANKSGIVING

Passages To Read Before You Pray:
Psalms 100, 118, 136

PRAYER POINTS:

1. Father Lord, I thank you because you are my God.
2. Father Lord, I thank you for the salvation of my soul, you sent your Son to die for me.
3. Father Lord, I thank you for rescuing me from the danger of Hell Fire.
4. Father Lord, I thank you for always being there for me.
5. Father Lord, I thank you for providing for all my needs.
6. Father Lord, I thank you for meeting all my needs.
7. Father Lord, I thank you for fighting all my battles.
8. Father Lord, I thank you for my good health and my families' good health.
9. Father Lord, I thank you for favor that I receive daily.
10. Father Lord, I thank you for protection over me and over my household.
11. Father Lord, I thank you for the mercies you extend to me everyday.
12. Father Lord, I thank you for the wonderful family that you have given me.
13. Father Lord, I thank you for your grace that is sufficient for me.
14. Father Lord, I thank you for the blood of Jesus that is available to me.
15. Father Lord, I thank you for the roof over my head.
16. Father Lord, I thank you for the food on my table.

17. Father Lord, I thank you for the gift of life and the breath in my nostrils.
18. Father Lord, I thank you for delivering me from the hands of the wicked.
19. Father Lord, I thank you for giving me your Holy Spirit .
20. Father Lord, I thank you for giving me the grace to know you.
21. Father Lord, I thank you for your Words that is guiding me and directing my path every day.
22. Father Lord, I thank you for keeping me from falling.
23. Father Lord, I thank you for all your promises for me and I know you will fulfill them.
24. Father Lord, I thank you for giving me a sound mind.
25. Father Lord, I thank you for being a good friend.
26. Father Lord, I thank you for your glory that covers and envelopes my life.
27. Father Lord, I thank you for wonderful things you are doing in my life, it is only you that could have done that.
28. Father Lord, I thank you for divine help that I receive every day.
29. Father Lord, I thank you for unfailing love toward me and my household
30. Father Lord, I thank you for keeping your Words that you have spoken concerning my life.
31. Father Lord, I thank you for good plans that you have for me.
32. Father Lord, I thank you for giving me a wonderful and bright future.
33. Father Lord, I thank you for surrounding me with your angels.
34. Father Lord, I thank you for giving me power and authority over devils and to cure diseases.
35. Father Lord, I thank you for forgiving my sins and washing me in the blood of Jesus.

36. Father Lord, I thank you for being my strongest tower and my great reward.
37. Father Lord, I thank you for giving me strength to go through every day.

HEARING THE VOICE OF GOD

Passages To Read Before You Pray:
Psalm 95, Hebrews 3:15

PRAYER POINTS:

1. Father Lord, I thank you for being my God, a wonderful Father and an awesome friend.
2. I thank you Lord, for the blood of Jesus that is available for me.
3. I confess before you O Lord, that I am a sinner, have mercy and forgive my sins.
4. According to your Word O Lord, cleanse me from all unrighteousness.
5. I cover myself in the blood of Jesus Christ.
6. Anything in my life hindering me from hearing your voice, Father Lord, remove it.
7. O God my father, talk to me, I want to hear from you.
8. I rebuke spiritual blindness that will not allow me to see the Lord.
9. Every spiritual blindness hindering me from seeing God, I cast you out of my life.
10. Every spiritual blindness hindering me from seeing the Shekinah Glory, I cast you out of my life.
11. Speak to me O Lord and direct my path in life.
12. Speak to me O Lord and order my footsteps in life.
13. Speak to me O Lord and instruct me about what to do in life.
14. Speak to me O Lord and give me hope in every hopeless area of my life.
15. Speak to me O Lord and give me solution to all my situations.
16. Speak to me O Lord, I want to fellowship with you.

17. Speak to me O Lord and confirm your Words in my life.
18. Speak to me O Lord and let your voice give me victory.
19. Speak to me O Lord and correct me when I am going astray.
20. Deafness in my spirit, I cast you out in Jesus name.
21. Spiritual deafness hindering me from hearing the voice of God, get out of my life.
22. O God my Father, let the loss of my spiritual hearing be restored.
23. My spiritual hearing that is malfunctioning, receive a touch from the Lord.
24. O God my Father, give me grace to recognize your voice when you speak.
25. O God my Father, give me grace to listen when you speak, so I will not miss your voice.
26. O God my Father, help me, I want to hear from you.
27. Problems of life that will not allow me to focus and listen when you speak, Father, let there be solution now.
28. Anxiety and needs that will not allow me to focus and listen when you speak, Father, let there be solution now.
29. Father Lord, give me grace to understand when you speak.
30. Every stony heart that will not allow me to hear your voice, Father, replaces it with heart of flesh.
31. Hardness of heart hindering me from hearing your voice, Father, break it now.
32. Every work of the flesh hindering me from hearing God's voice, I cast you out of my life.
33. Every spirit of unbelief hindering me from hearing God's voice, I cast you out of my life.
34. Every spiritual laziness, hindering me from hearing God's Voice, I cast you out of my life.
35. Every spirit of stubbornness, hindering me from hearing God's voice, I cast you out of my life in the name of Jesus.
36. Father Lord, let my spiritual antenna function normally.

37. Father Lord, let my spiritual ear be flushed and cleansed by the blood of Jesus.
38. I receive divine connection today, Father Lord, I will always hear your voice when you speak.
39. Father Lord, give me discerning spirit to know the difference between your voice and the voices of the enemy.
40. O God my Father, speak and let your voice give me comfort.
41. O God my Father, speak and let your voice give me boldness to confront any situation in my life.
42. O God my Father, speak into every area of my life, so the whole world may know that I serve the living God.

BREAKING EVIL CYCLE

Passages To Read Before You Pray:
Psalms 6, 9, 46, 105, 106, Mark 5:25-34

PRAYER POINTS:

1. Father Lord, I thank you because you are the Lord God of all flesh, and nothing is impossible unto you.
2. In any area that I am falling short of your glory, Father forgive me and show me mercy in the name of Jesus Christ.
3. I cover myself and my household in the blood of Jesus.
4. By the power in the name of Jesus, I break every evil cycle in my life.
5. Every cycle of pain manifesting in my life, break in the name of Jesus Christ.
6. O God my Father, send your fire to the foundation of the cycle of pain in my life and destroy it.
7. Every cycle of shame manifesting in my life, break in the name of Jesus Christ.
8. O God my Father, send your fire and destroy the cycle of shame from the foundation in the name of Jesus Christ.
9. Every cycle of sickness manifesting in my life, break in the name of Jesus Christ.
10. O God my Father, send your fire and destroy the cycle of sickness from the foundation in the name of Jesus Christ.
11. Every cycle of failure manifesting in my life, break in the name of Jesus Christ.
12. O God my Father, send your fire and destroy the cycle of failure from the foundation in the name of Jesus Christ.
13. Every cycle of poverty manifesting in my life, break in the name of Jesus Christ.

14. O God my Father, send your fire and destroy the cycle of poverty from the foundation in the name of Jesus Christ.
15. Every cycle of disappointment manifesting in my life, break in the name of Jesus Christ.
16. O God my Father, send your fire and destroy the cycle of disappointment from the foundation in the name of Jesus Christ.
17. Every cycle of tears manifesting in my life, break in the name of Jesus Christ.
18. O God my Father, send your fire and destroy the cycle of tears from the foundation in the name of Jesus Christ.
19. Every cycle of backwardness manifesting in my life, break in the name of Jesus Christ.
20. O God my Father, send your fire and destroy the cycle of backwardness from the foundation in the name of Jesus Christ.
21. Every cycle of demotion manifesting in my life, break in the name of Jesus Christ.
22. O God my Father, send your fire and destroy the cycle of demotion from the foundation in the name of Jesus Christ.
23. Every cycle of misfortune manifesting in my life, break in the name of Jesus Christ.
24. O God my Father, send your fire and destroy the cycle of misfortune from the foundation in the name of Jesus Christ.
25. Every cycle of loneliness manifesting in my life, break in the name of Jesus Christ.
26. O God my Father, send your fire and destroy the cycle of loneliness from the foundation in the name of Jesus Christ.
27. Every cycle of disgrace manifesting in my life, break in the name of Jesus Christ.
28. O God my Father, send your fire and destroy the cycle of disgrace from the foundation in the name of Jesus Christ.

29. Every cycle of demonic attack manifesting in my life, break in the name of Jesus Christ.

30. O God my Father, send your fire and destroy the cycle of demonic attack from the foundation in the name of Jesus Christ.

31. Every cycle of rejection manifesting in my life, break in the name of Jesus Christ.

32. O God my Father, send your fire and destroy the cycle of rejection from the foundation in the name of Jesus Christ.

33. Every cycle of drought manifesting in my life, break in the name of Jesus Christ.

34. Every cycle of drought manifesting in my business, break in the name of Jesus Christ.

35. Every cycle of drought manifesting in my finances, break in the name of Jesus Christ.

36. O God my Father, send your fire and destroy the cycle of drought from the foundation in the name of Jesus Christ.

37. Every cycle of confusion manifesting in my life, break in the name of Jesus Christ.

38. O God my Father, send your fire and destroy the cycle of confusion from the foundation in the name of Jesus Christ.

39. Every cycle of misfortune manifesting in my life, break in the name of Jesus Christ.

40. O God my Father, send your fire and destroy the cycle of misfortune from the foundation in the name of Jesus Christ.

41. Every cycle of suffering manifesting in my life, break in the name of Jesus Christ.

42. O God my Father, send your fire and destroy the cycle of suffering from the foundation in the name of Jesus Christ.

43. Every cycle of limitation manifesting in my life, break in the name of Jesus Christ.

44. O God my Father, send your fire and destroy the cycle of limitation from the foundation in the name of Jesus Christ.

45. Every cycle of limitation manifesting in my family, break in the name of Jesus Christ.
46. Every cycle of limitation manifesting in my business, break in the name of Jesus Christ.
47. Every cycle of ridicule manifesting in my life, break in the name of Jesus Christ.
48. Every cycle of ridicule manifesting in my family, break in the name of Jesus Christ.
49. O God my Father, send your fire and destroy the cycle of ridicule from the foundation in the name of Jesus Christ.
50. Every cycle of spiritual blindness manifesting in my life, break in the name of Jesus Christ.

I CAN MOVE MOUNTAIN

Passages To Read Before You Pray:
Psalms 30, 46, Zechariah 4:7, Matthew 17:20

PRAYER POINTS:

1. Father Lord, I thank you for being a wonderful God and an awesome friend.
2. Anything that I have done that can hinder the move of God in my life, Father Lord, forgive me and cleanse me in the blood of Jesus Christ.
3. O God my Father, fill me with the anointing and the power of the Holy Ghost.
4. Every evil mountain blocking my miracles, I command you to be removed in the name of Jesus Christ.
5. Every evil mountain blocking my open heavens, I command you to be removed in the name of Jesus Christ.
6. Every evil mountain blocking my breakthroughs, I command you to be removed in the name of Jesus Christ.
7. Every evil mountain blocking my progress, be removed now in the name of Jesus Christ.
8. Every evil mountain blocking my blessings, be removed now in the name of Jesus Christ.
9. Every evil mountain blocking my success, be removed now in the name of Jesus Christ.
10. Every mountain of impossibility confronting me, be removed now in the name of Jesus Christ.
11. Every mountain of unbelief confronting me, be removed now in the name of Jesus Christ.
12. Every mountain of poverty confronting me, be removed now in the name of Jesus Christ.

13. Every mountain of stagnancy in my life, be removed now in the name of Jesus Christ.
14. Every mountain of failure in my life, be removed now in the name of Jesus Christ.
15. Every mountain of confusion confronting me, get out of my way in the name of Jesus Christ.
16. Every evil mountain of sickness and infirmity, get out of my life in the name of Jesus Christ.
17. Every mountain of backwardness holding my life back, loose your hold upon me now in the name of Jesus Christ.
18. Every mountain of barrenness delaying my fruitfulness, loose your hold over my life in the name of Jesus Christ.
19. Every mountain of loneliness in my life, be removed and be destroyed in the name of Jesus Christ.
20. Every mountain of bad luck confronting me, be destroyed in the name of Jesus Christ.
21. Evil mountain of satanic attack, be removed now in the name of Jesus Christ.
22. Every mountain of shame confronting me, be removed in the name of Jesus Christ.
23. Every mountain of ridicule manifesting in my life, be removed in the name of Jesus Christ.
24. Every mountain of disappointment confronting me, be removed in the name of Jesus Christ.
25. Every mountain of disapproval delaying my progress, be removed in the name of Jesus Christ.
26. Every mountain of rejection confronting me, be removed in the name of Jesus Christ.
27. Every mountain of almost there holding back my breakthroughs, be removed now in the name of Jesus Christ.
28. Every mountain of financial failure planning to put me to shame, be removed now in the name of Jesus Christ.

29. Every mountain of business failure confronting my business, be removed now in the name of Jesus Christ.
30. Every mountain of marital problem confronting my marriage, be removed now in the name of Jesus Christ.
31. Every mountain of satanic dreams turning my sleep into battle ground, be removed and be destroyed in the name of Jesus Christ.
32. Every mountain of ancestral problems, be removed now in the name of Jesus Christ.
33. Every mountain of generational curses manifesting in my life, be removed now in the name of Jesus Christ.
34. Every mountain of financial drought, be removed now in the name of Jesus Christ.
35. Every mountain created by evil pronouncement, be removed and be destroyed in the name of Jesus Christ.
36. Every mountain of depression manifesting in my life, be destroyed in the name of Jesus Christ.
37. Every mountain of frustration manifesting in my life, be destroyed in the name of Jesus Christ.
38. Every mountain of fear manifesting in my life, be destroyed now in the name of Jesus Christ.
39. Every mighty mountain hindering me from entering my promise land, be destroyed by the fire of God.
40. Every mighty mountain standing between me and my miracles, be destroyed by the fire of God.
41. Every mountain of delay manifesting in my life, be destroyed by the fire of God.
42. Every mountain of limitation confronting me, be destroyed by the fire of God.
43. O God my Father, increase my faith and help my unbelief in the name of Jesus Christ.

IT SHALL WORK FOR MY GOOD

Passages To Read Before You Pray:
Genesis 37:18-20; 39:3-6; 49:25; 50:20, Romans 8:28

PRAYER PONITS

1. Father Lord, I thank you for standing by your Words in my life.
2. Father Lord, forgive me of anything that I have done against your will.
3. From this moment O Lord, let everything work together for my good.
4. Every evil plan of the enemy shall turn around and work together for my good.
5. Every work of the devil against me shall turn around and work together for my good.
6. Every work of the devil against my progress shall turn around and work together to accelerate my progress.
7. Every work of the devil against my finances, turn around and work together to produce abundance in my finances.
8. Every work of the devil against my breakthroughs shall turn around and work together for my breakthrough.
9. Every work of the devil against my joy shall turn around and work together to increase my joy.
10. Every work of the devil against my destiny shall turn around and work together to fulfill my destiny.
11. Every work of the devil against my dreams shall turn around and work together to fulfill my dream.
12. Every work of the devil against my home shall turn around and work together to bring me joy.

13. Every work of the devil against my children shall turn around and work together to fulfill my children's purpose in life.
14. Every evil counsel against me shall work together for my good.
15. Every evil decision made against me shall work together for my good.
16. Every evil idea raised against me shall work together for my good.
17. Every evil collaboration against me shall work together for my good.
18. Every evil network built against me shall work together for my good.
19. Every evil meeting held against me shall work together for my good.
20. I command heavens to open and release blessings of heaven to me.
21. I command heaven to open and release my breakthroughs to me.
22. I command heaven to open and release abundance into my life.
23. I command heaven to open and release unusual favor into my life.
24. I command heaven to open and release my miracles.
25. I command heaven to open and release my healing.
26. I command heaven to open and release my joy.
27. I command heaven to open and let latter rain and former rain be released upon me.
28. I command heaven to open and release my promotion.
29. Arise O God and connect me with my helpers.
30. Arise O God and lead me to my promise land.
31. Arise O God and deliver me from the hands of the wicked.
32. O God arise and kill my Pharaoh.
33. O God arise and destroy my Goliath.

34. O God arise and take away my reproach.
35. O God arise and take away my shame.
36. O God arise and fulfill your promises in my life.
37. O God arise and fight my battles.
38. O God arise and demonstrate your power in my life.
39. I command heaven to open and release heavenly treasures into my life .
40. I command heaven to open and change my destiny for the best.
41. O God my Father, open up the deep and let my blessings be released.
42. O God my Father, open up the deep and let my buried glory be released.
43. O God my Father, open up the deep and let my dreams come alive.
44. O God my Father, open up the deep and let my stolen miracles be restored to me.
45. O God my Father, open up the deep and let my dead stars come alive.
46. O God my Father, open up the deep and let my joy be released.
47. O God my Father, open up the deep and let my hindered blessings be released.
48. O God my Father, open up the deep and let my promotion be confirmed.
49. O God my Father, open up the deep and let my success be released.
50. O God my Father, open up the deep and let my stagnated life move forward.
51. I receive the grace of God to complete every good thing I lay my hands on.
52. I receive the grace of God to succeed in all my good efforts in this year.

53. Every day of my life I shall be productive.
54. Every minute of my life shall bring me harvest.
55. In my life, I shall not labor in vain.
56. As from this moment, wealth and riches shall locate me and be my friend.
57. Every satanic attack against my finances, go back to sender.
58. Every satanic attack against my home, go back to sender.
59. Every satanic attack against my joy, go back to sender.
60. Every satanic attack sent to frustrate me, go back to sender.

PRAYER AGAINST MISCARRIAGE

Passages To Read Before You Pray:
Exodus 23:26, Deuteronomy 7:14-15, Psalms 60, 113

PRAYER POINTS:

1. Every power delaying my change of status from lady to mother, loose your hold over my life in the name of Jesus Christ.
2. Every power causing me to lose my pregnancy, you no longer permitted to do so, loose your hold over my life in the name of Jesus Christ.
3. Every timed or programmed sickness that always happen to me during pregnancy, you are no longer allowed, loose your hold over my life in the name of Jesus Christ.
4. Every power that has set limit on how far my pregnancy can grow, you will not prosper in the name of Jesus Christ.
5. Every power that always attack me with different kinds of sickness and ailment during pregnancy, you are no longer allowed, loose your hold over my life in the name of Jesus Christ.
6. Whatever God gives, He does not take back, I receive grace to carry my pregnancy successfully in the name of Jesus Christ.
7. I cover myself in the blood of Jesus Christ, I shall no longer lose my pregnancy in the name of Jesus Christ.
8. O my womb, I command you in the name of Jesus Christ, receive strength to hold babies.
9. O my womb, I command you in the name of Jesus Christ, receive healing wherever healing is needed.

10. O my womb, reject every curse of miscarriage in the name of Jesus Christ.
11. I reject premature delivery, I shall carry my baby to the full term in the name of Jesus Christ.
12. Devil you are a liar, God is on my side, I shall no longer lose any pregnancy in the name of Jesus Christ.
13. Every power that wants me to feel my baby but will not allow me to hold him/her, I bind you and render you powerless over me and my baby in the name of Jesus Christ.
14. Every power that wants me to see my baby but will not allow me to touch him/her, I bind you and render you powerless over me and my baby in the name of Jesus Christ.
15. Every power that wants me to touch my baby but will not allow me to keep him/her, I bind you and render you powerless over me and my baby in the name of Jesus Christ.
16. Every power that wants me to keep my baby but will not allow me to enjoy him/her, I bind you and render you powerless over me and my baby in the name of Jesus Christ.
17. Every power that wants me to suffer by losing my babies, I am no longer your victim, I bind you and render you powerless over me and my babies in the name of Jesus Christ.
18. Every self inflicted problem causing miscarriage in my pregnancies, receive solution today in the name of Jesus Christ.
19. Every mark of the enemy upon my life causing miscarriage in my pregnancies, be erased by the blood of Jesus Christ.
20. Every power that has received mandate to let me conceive but will not let me have baby, you will not prosper, loose you hold over me in the name of Jesus Christ.

BABY DELIVERY

Passages To Read Before You Pray:
Exodus 1:15-19, Psalm 42

PRAYER POINTS:

1. Father Lord, I thank you for the blessing of the womb.
2. Father Lord, I thank you for the grace upon me to bring your wonderful gift to life.
3. If there is anything that I have done in the process of conception against your will, forgive me Lord.
4. O God my Father, let the anointing of Hebrew women rest upon me at the point of baby delivery.
5. I reject painful delivery, I receive anointing for easy and smooth delivery.
6. By the authority in the name of Jesus Christ, I cancel every complication concerning my baby delivery.
7. By the authority in the name of Jesus Christ, I reject premature baby delivery.
8. By the authority in the name of Jesus Christ, I will carry my baby to the full term.
9. By the power in the name of Jesus Christ, my baby delivery will not be delayed.
10. I reject body weakness and tiredness, I receive strength from the Lord to deliver my baby.
11. O God my Father, doctors, nurses and midwives that will attend to me, give them wisdom and grace to deliver my baby safely.
12. I cancel every evil plan of the enemy against my baby delivery.

13. The day of my baby delivery shall be a day of joy and thanksgiving.
14. O God my Father, fill the delivery room with your presence.
15. O God my Father, dispatch your angels to come and work with doctors, nurses and midwives that will deliver my baby.
16. By the authority in the name of Jesus Christ, I command my baby to be in the right position for delivery.
17. By the authority in the name of Jesus Christ, I command every part and organ in my body to function well for my baby delivery.
18. My baby shall breath well and be in good health before and after the delivery.
19. I will be in good health before and after my baby delivery.
20. O God my Father, take all the glory to yourself and fill my heart with great joy.
21. Before I bend, I will deliver safely.
22. I reject sickness before and after my baby delivery.
23. I reject complication before and after my baby delivery.
24. Father Lord, let my baby be filled with the Holy Ghost from the womb.
25. I reject long and painful labor, my baby delivery shall be quick, easy and safe.

SEED OF GREATNESS

Passages To Read Before You Pray:
Genesis 12:2-3, 17:6-8, 21:18, 22:16-18, 26:3-4, 12-13; Deuteronomy 28:2-14

PRAYER POINTS:

1. Father Lord, I thank you for giving me the gift of life, and for your Holy Spirit in me.
2. O God my Father, forgive me of all my sins and cleanse me in the blood of Jesus Christ.
3. O God my Father, fill me with your Holy Spirit and let every work of the flesh in me die.
4. Every seed of greatness deposited in me, begin to grow in the name of Jesus Christ.
5. Every seed of greatness deposited in me, manifest by fire in the name of Jesus Christ.
6. Every cloud of doubt covering my greatness, disappear in the name of Jesus Christ.
7. Every cloud of unbelief covering my greatness, disappear in the name of Jesus Christ.
8. Every cloud of darkness covering my greatness, disappear by fire in the name of Jesus Christ.
9. Every cloud of hatred covering my greatness, disappear in the name of Jesus Christ.
10. Every cloud of almost there covering my greatness, disappear in the name of Jesus.
11. You seed of greatness in me, come out now without delay in the name of Jesus Christ.
12. O God my Father, let my greatness be revealed to the world.

13. Any power fighting against my greatness, you will not escape the judgment of God.
14. Any power hindering my greatness, you will not escape the judgment of God.
15. I receive the anointing and the grace of God, I will spread to the south, to the north, to the east and to the west in the name of Jesus Christ.
16. I receive the grace and the anointing to possess the gates of my enemies in the name of Jesus Christ.
17. O God my Father, let my greatness come out like sunrise in the morning time.
18. If no one can hinder the sun from rising, no power can hinder my greatness in the name of Jesus Christ.
19. If no one can stop the sun from shining, no power will be able to stop my greatness in the name of Jesus Christ.
20. No matter the activity and the efforts of the enemies, I will be great on earth in the name of Jesus Christ.
21. Every evil network working against my greatness, scatter by the fire of God.
22. Every evil network working against the plan of God for my life, scatter by the fire of God.
23. I receive anointing and the grace of God to be a blessing to this generation and generations to come in the name of Jesus Christ.
24. O God my Father, make my name great according to your Word.
25. O God my Father, make me a great blessing to my family in the name of Jesus Christ.
26. Anyone that blesses me, Father Lord bless them; and anyone that curses me shall be cursed in the name of Jesus Christ.
27. Any plan of the enemy to delay the manifestation of my greatness, be aborted in the name of Jesus Christ.

28. Any plan of the enemy to terminate my greatness, be cancelled in the name of Jesus Christ.

29. Any plan of the enemy to contaminate the divine agenda for my life, be disappointed in the name of Jesus Christ.

30. Any plan of the enemy to change the divine agenda for my life, be disappointed in the name of Jesus Christ.

31. Any plan contrary to the plan of God for my life, be cancelled in the name of Jesus Christ.

32. I cover the seed of greatness in me in the blood of Jesus Christ.

33. I baptize the seed of greatness deposited in me in the fire of the Holy Ghost.

34. O God my Father, people that you have ordained to contribute to the manifestation of my greatness, let them locate me in the name of Jesus Christ.

35. Any plan of the enemy to use me against myself, be disappointed in the name of Jesus Christ.

36. My greatness shall not be postponed in the name of Jesus Christ.

37. My greatness shall not be transferred to another man, in the name of Jesus Christ.

38. My greatness shall not be contaminated.

39. My greatness shall not be terminated.

40. My greatness will not die, my greatness will manifest and become a reality in the name of Jesus Christ.

DRY BONES SHALL LIVE

Passages To Read Before You Pray:
Psalm 18, Proverbs 18:21, Ezekiel 37:1-12

PRAYER POINTS:

1. Father Lord, I thank you because you are God of possibility and there is nothing impossible for you.
2. O God my Father, forgive me of my past mistakes and errors in the name of Jesus Christ.
3. O God my Father, let your mighty hands rest upon me for miracles, breakthroughs, healing and deliverance.
4. O God my Father, let your mighty hands carry me out of where I am to where you want me to be.
5. O God my Father, let my valley of dry bones be converted to mountain of testimonies.
6. Father Lord, you are the hope for the hopeless, let my lost hope be restored.
7. Today O Lord, do the impossible in every area of my life and let my dry bones receive the life of God and live.
8. O God my Father, let every dry bone in every area of my life receive the life of God and live.
9. O God my Father, let my dead dreams receive the life of God and live.
10. O God my Father, let my dead potential receive the life of God and live.
11. O God my Father, let my dead glory receive the life of God and live.
12. O God my Father, let my dead business receive the life of God and live.

13. O God my Father, let every dead organ in my body receive the life of God and live.
14. O God my Father, let my dead star receive the life of God and live.
15. I speak life into every organ in my body.
16. I speak life into my life and destiny.
17. I speak life into my finances.
18. I speak life into the life of my wife/husband.
19. I speak life into marriage.
20. I speak life into the life of my children.
21. I speak life into my business and my sources of income.
22. I speak life into my dreams and my future.
23. O God my Father, stretch out your mighty hands and restore my joy.
24. O God my Father, stretch out your mighty hands and restore my glory.
25. O God my Father, stretch out your mighty hands and restore my lost miracles.
26. O God my Father, stretch out your mighty hands and restore my lost opportunities.
27. O God my Father, stretch out your mighty hands and restore my lost blessings.
28. O God my Father, stretch out your mighty hands and convert my failure to success.
29. O God my Father, stretch out your mighty hands and convert my ridicules to miracles.
30. O God my Father, stretch out your mighty hands and convert my trials to triumph.
31. O God my Father, stretch out your mighty hands and convert my tests to testimonies.
32. O God my Father, stretch out your mighty hands and convert barrenness to fruitfulness.

33. O God my Father, stretch out your mighty hands and convert my stagnated life to progressive life.
34. O God my Father, stretch out your mighty hands and convert my demotion to promotion.
35. O God my Father, stretch out your mighty hands and convert my tears to laughter.
36. O God my Father, stretch out your mighty hands and convert my misfortune to good fortune and favor.
37. I command my situation to cooperate with the plan of God for my life.
38. I command every circumstance around me to cooperate with divine agenda for my life.
39. O God my father, let there be a shaking and let my life be restored.
40. O God my father, let there be a shaking and let my blessings be released.
41. I speak solution into every unpleasant situation in my life.
42. I speak solution into every stubborn situation in my life.
43. I speak " Let there be Light" into every darkness in any area of my life.
44. I speak peace be still into every stormy situation in my life.
45. I claim victory over every battle against my life.

I REJECT POVERTY

Passages To Read Before You Pray:
2 Kings 4:1-7, Philippians 4:19, Psalm 115:12-16, Deuteronomy 28:12

PRAYER POINTS:

1. Father Lord, I thank you for being my provider and my source of joy.
2. I confess my sins before you O Lord, forgive me and cleanse me in the blood of Jesus Christ.
3. I cover myself and my household in the blood of Jesus Christ.
4. Every curse of poverty upon my life, break by the fire of God.
5. Every spirit of poverty assigned against my family line, I am no longer under your bondage, loose your hold upon my life in the name of Jesus Christ.
6. Spirit of poverty working against my finances, I am no longer under your bondage, loose your hold upon my life in the name of Jesus Christ.
7. Spirit of poverty working against the divine agenda for my life, I am no longer under your bondage, loose your hold upon me now in the name of Jesus Christ.
8. Spirit of poverty working against my dreams, get out of my life now and never come back in the name of Jesus Christ.
9. Spirit of poverty working against my sources of income, get out of my life now and never come back in the name of Jesus Christ.
10. Spirit of poverty working against my good efforts, get out of my life now and never come back in the name of Jesus Christ.

11. Poverty transferred into my life, you are no longer allowed to stay, get out now and never come back in the name of Jesus Christ.

12. Poverty entered into my life as a result of my past mistake, I have been forgiven, you no longer have the right to be in my life, get out now and never come back in Jesus' name.

13. Poverty entered into my life as a result of bad association, get out of my life now and never come back in the name of Jesus Christ.

14. Poverty entered into my life as a result of disobedience, I have repented and been set free, get out of my life now and never come back in the name of Jesus Christ.

15. Poverty entered into my life as a result of evil pronouncement, get out of my life now and never come back in the name of Jesus Christ.

16. Poverty entered into my life as a result of unbelief, get out of my life and never come back in the name of Jesus Christ.

17. Poverty entered into my life as a result of my lifestyle, get out of my life and never come back in the name of Jesus Christ.

18. Poverty entered into my life because of another man's mistake, get out of my life and never come back in the name of Jesus Christ.

19. Poverty entered into my life as a result of my parents' mistakes, get out of my life and never come back in the name of Jesus Christ.

20. Poverty entered into my life as a result of bad decisions, get out of my life and never come back in the name of Jesus Christ.

21. With all my heart, I reject poverty in the name of Jesus Christ.

22. Evil mark of poverty upon my life, be removed by the blood of Jesus Christ.

23. Every arrow of poverty shot at me, go back to sender in the name of Jesus Christ.
24. Any power attacking me with poverty, carry your own evil load in the name of Jesus Christ.
25. Today O Lord, open my heavens of prosperity.
26. Today O Lord, open my heavens of financial blessings.
27. Today O Lord, open my heavens of abundance.
28. Today O Lord, open the heavens of my breakthroughs.
29. Today O Lord, open unto me divine source of supply.
30. O God my Father, supply all my needs according to your Word in the name of Jesus Christ.
31. O God my Father, release abundance into my life today in the name of Jesus Christ.
32. O God my Father, release surplus into my life today in the name of Jesus Christ.
33. Release into my life O Lord, blessings that will put poverty to shame in my life in the name of Jesus Christ.
34. My source of supply will never run dry in the name of Jesus Christ.
35. Poverty will never be mentioned in my household again in the name of Jesus Christ.
36. Inherited poverty, you are not allowed in any area of my life in the name of Jesus Christ.
37. I receive the grace and power of God to overcome poverty and lack in the name of Jesus Christ.
38. With the grace of God upon me, I claim and receive financial and material blessings in the name of Jesus Christ.
39. With the grace of God upon me, I claim riches and wealth designed and prepared for me in the name of Jesus Christ.
40. With the grace of God upon me, I claim milk and honey flowing in this land in the name of Jesus Christ.
41. I will be rich and not be poor in the name of Jesus Christ.

42. I will have everything in abundance and lack nothing in the name of Jesus Christ.
43. I claim everything that belongs to me, I shall miss nothing in the name of Jesus Christ.
44. O God my Father, let the riches and wealth from every corner of the earth locate me in the name of Jesus Christ.
45. I will be the lender and shall not borrow in the name of Jesus Christ.

SPEAKING INTO THE NEW MONTH

Passages To Read Before You Pray:
Isaiah 43:19, Joel 2:21-24, Habakkuk 1:5

PRAYER POINTS

1. I command this new month to cooperate with divine agenda for my life.
2. I command this month to cooperate with divine agenda for my spouse.
3. I command this new month to cooperate with divine agenda for my children.
4. You month of _____ (*mention the name of the month*), you will not work against me.
5. Every minute of this new month will favor me.
6. Every situation in this new month will favor me.
7. Every situation in this new month will work together for my good.
8. My blessings shall multiply in the month of _____ .
9. In this new month, my joy shall be full.
10. From the beginning of this new month to the end, I shall operate under the anointing of increase.
11. From the beginning of this new month to the end, I shall operate under open heavens.
12. From the beginning of this new month to the end, I shall enjoy the goodness of the Lord.
13. Anointing for unusual favor in the month of _____ , fall upon me without measure.
14. In this new month, I will rise from minimum to maximum.

15. From the beginning of this new month to the end, I will live in abundance.
16. From the beginning of this new month to the end, I will live in prosperity.
17. From the beginning of this new month to the end, I shall lack nothing.
18. O God my Father, let my harvest begin now and never stop.
19. With the power of life in my tongue, I speak increase into every area of my life.
20. With the power of life in my tongue, I speak increase into my harvest.
21. I speak increase into my finances.
22. In this new month O Lord, let doors of opportunity continually open upon me.
23. O God my Father, let every minute of this month in my life be filled with joy and happiness.
24. O God my Father, let every minute of this month in my life be filled with testimonies.
25. O Go my Father, let every minute of this month in my life be filled with thanksgiving.
26. I cover every minute of my life in this new month with the blood of Jesus.
27. In the month of _____, my prayers shall produce results.
28. I receive strength and grace to fulfill purpose in the month of _____.
29. In this new month, my glory will not sink and my dreams will not die.
30. I will rise and I will shine in the month of _____.
31. In this month, I will be the head and not the tail.
32. In this month, I will be above only and not beneath.
33. In this month, I will be the lender and not the borrower.
34. The time of walking and running is over, I receive the anointing to fly high in the month of _____.

35. In this month, I will mount up with wings as an eagle.
36. In this month, I will live on the mountaintop and not in the valley.
37. O God my Father, in this new month, my life shall bring glory to your name.
38. O God my Father, in this new month, works of my hands shall bring you joy.
39. O God my Father, give me grace so that I will not disappoint you in this new month.
40. In the month of _____, Father, let my life and my home reflect your glory.

LET THERE BE LIGHT

Passages To Read Before You Pray:
Genesis 1:1-28, Psalms 19, 29, 42

PRAYER POINTS:

1. O God my Father, speak let there be light to every darkness in my life.
2. O God my Father, speak let there be light into every darkness in my way.
3. O God my Father, speak let there be light into every darkness covering my destiny.
4. O God my Father, speak let there be light into every hiding place of the enemy in my life.
5. O God my Father, speak let there be light into anything in my life that is harboring darkness.
6. O God my Father, speak let there be light and let every work of darkness in my life disappear.
7. O God my Father, speak let there be light to every darkness covering my vision.
8. O God my Father, speak let there be light to every darkness covering my glory.
9. O God my Father, speak let there be light and let darkness in my home flee.
10. O God my Father, speak let there be light and let every work of darkness in my life tremble.
11. O God my Father, speak calmness into every storm of my life.
12. O God my Father, speak calmness into every stubborn situation in my life.

13. O God my Father, speak calmness into every situation that wants to swallow me up.
14. O God my Father, speak calmness into every evil storm in my home.
15. O God my Father, speak calmness into every evil storm in my business.
16. O God my Father, speak calmness into every evil storm in my finances.
17. O God my Father, speak calmness into every destructive storms rising against my finances.
18. O God my Father, speak calmness to every destructive storm rising against my family.
19. O God my Father, speak calmness to every destructive storm that wants to destroy my dreams.
20. O God my Father, speak calmness to every storm that wants to destroy everything that I have worked for.
21. O God my Father, speak calmness to every storm that wants me to labor in vain.
22. O God my Father, speak calmness into every storm creating fear in my life.
23. O God my Father, speak solution to every stubborn situation in my life.
24. O God my Father, speak solution to the financial embarrassment that I am going through.
25. O God my Father, speak solution to every fruitless job hunting in my life.
26. O God my Father, speak solution to every hard labor less blessing in my life.
27. O God my Father, speak solution to vain labor in my life.
28. O God my Father, speak solution to every unrepentant situation in my life.
29. O God my Father, speak solution to every hopeless situation in my life.

30. O God my Father, speak let there be a solution to every confusing stage of my life.
31. O God my Father, speak let there be a solution to every stubborn situation in my home.
32. O God my Father, speak let there be a solution to every situation that makes me cry.

AUTHOR

 Tim Atunnise is the senior pastor of Global Vision Ministries Inc in Atlanta- Georgia, USA. He was called into ministry at the age of 23 as a pastor, prophet and dynamic teacher of the Word.

Atunnise believes that you must discover the anointing and power of God within you, realize that you have everything you need to fulfill your God-given destiny, and stand on God's promises, protecting them at all costs with the power of prayer.

Tim Atunnise is a highly sought-after counselor, business consultant and entrepreneurial trainer. This is a story of what is possible for those who love God and are called according to His purpose (Romans 8:28).

Atunnise spent an impoverished childhood in Nigeria. From the trials and triumphs, you will learn the power of vision, responsibility, integrity and faithfulness. More importantly, you will know beyond a doubt that with God, all things are possible (Matthew 19:26).

He is the author of "Prayer of The Day" and many other books.

Tim Atunnise is happily married to Becky, and blessed with 2 wonderful boys, Timothy and Joseph.

Other books written by Tim Atunnise:

- Prayer of The Day – Volume I
- Prayer of The Day – Volume II
- Prayer of The Day – Volume III
- Prayer of The Day – Volume IV
- Overcoming Self (Sunday School Manual)
- Overcoming Self (Teacher's Copy)
- The Parables (Sunday School Manual)
- The Parables (Teacher's Copy)
- The Fruits of the Spirit (Sunday School Manual)
- The Fruits of the Spirit (Teacher's Copy)
- The Book of Daniel Made Easy
- Divine Prescriptions
- I Must Win This Battle (Personal Deliverance)
- Lost & Found: The House of Israel

Notes

Made in the USA
Lexington, KY
03 May 2015